ngratulations to Dan and Manon Rodriguez for writing a book that is great help to lots of people. It's a must-read if you want to improve your mmunications and business partnership skills.

~ Jane C. Willhite, CEO, PSI Seminars

extraordinary book! Dan and Manon Rodriguez are masters of business tnerships. Apply the information in this book and you can be a master too!

~ Gerry Robert, president, LifeSuccess Publishing,
author of The *Millionaire Mindset*

low the advice in this book and you will definitely get your business on right track.

~ Allan J. Katz, LoyaltyCoach.com,
author of *Addictive Entrepreneurship*

thing with Two Heads is a Freak is a "must have" publication for anyone who lanning to start their own business or improve their existing business. Dan Manon Rodriguez thoroughly enlighten readers as to what to expect when ering into a partnership. After reading this book you will be hard-pressed to any surprises with your partnership. This book will serve as a valuable prep erial and an even better reference guide.

~ Laraine Russo Harper, author of *Legal Tender*

n and intelligent read! This tell-all book shakes up the current perception of ness partnerships. Wait until the media gets a hold of this one.

~ Jeff Crilley, RealNewsPR.com, author of *Free Publicity*

Further Acclaim for

Anything With Two Heads Is

Dan and Manon Rodriguez are protégé students of mine. Th full of excellent ideas and proven partnership strategies that w in your business. I recommend you buy two copies of this bo one for your partner.

~ Robert G. Allen, co-founder, Enlightene
bestselling autho

This book is a *homerun*! It reflects the talent, insight and Manon possess. It is not only interesting reading, but a t who have the desire to own a business and be their own bos

~ George Strike, partn

The many tools and techniques described in this book will s and frustration. Dan and Manon Rodriguez are not writing theoretical point of view. It is evident they live what they w

~ Bob Proctor, star of *The Secret*, author o

This book is required reading if you want to create effective *partnerships.* My brother Robert has been my business partner for most of my career. We have diverging skills and opinions on many subjects. Yet, our strong *partnership* has been the key to both our success. Neither could have succeeded without the other. If you aspire to be a millionaire entrepreneur - read this book!

~ Richard Garriott, astronaut and millionaire entrepreneur

Every business person should own a copy of *Anything with Two Heads is a Freak*. The information is priceless and you will find yourself referring back to the book often. I admire the authors—-and so will you.

~ Lucy Ivins, corporate leadership coach

Dan and Manon have revealed the secrets of succeeding in business through the partnerships you create. Apply the teachings and it all becomes possible. This book works like *magic!*

~ George Schindler, Dean, Society of American Magicians

Dan and Manon have written an amazing book that teaches you the science of creating successful business partnerships.

~Steve Spangler, TV host, science education specialist, and author

Anything with Two Heads is a Freak is an excellent book for the entrepreneur in the making. It teaches proven and tested principles that will support your business and financial goals.

~ Loral Langemeier, author of *The Millionaire Maker*

The authors got it! This book has the vision and the purpose of a real partnership. You'll learn the 'why' and proven information we can all apply to our businesses and lives to create success.

~ Keith Froehling, inspirational speaker, bestselling author

This book is an incredible resource for business owners, managers, and trainers. Read it and you will have the tools to attract excellent business partnerships.

~ Rebecca Hanson, founder of the Law of Attraction Training Center, author

Recommended reading for all home-based business owners. The goal setting and communication strategies in this book will put your business on the fast track to success.

~ Alan Pariser, Corporate Director V, Melaleuca Inc.,
founder of AdvancingWithUs.com

The KEY to succeeding in business partnerships is locked between the pages of this book. You have a treasure of knowledge in your possession.

~ Dr. Joe Vitale, featured in *The Secret*, author of *The Attractor Factor*

Getting more out of business partnerships is magically unveiled in this book. *Anything with Two Heads is a Freak* gives you the tools to lead yourself to greater success in business.

~ Frank Kickbush, author of *The Secrets of Self-Leadership*

This book is a treasure trove of principles, methods, concepts, techniques, and ideas that will change your business life. I recommend you buy this book and do what it says.

~ Anita Selby, recreation therapist, author of *Re-Create the Senior's Soul*

Anything with Two Heads is a Freak is rich in content and easy to read. If you own a business, I suggest you buy this book and read it cover-to-cover.

~ Shawn Shewchuk, success coach,
author of *Change Your Mind, Change Your Results!*

This book tackles the complex issue of partnerships and simplifies it into actionable steps. A very good read!

~ Doug Meharg, author of *Become a Richer You*

This book is *well packaged!* I have applied many of the partnering strategies in my business and I am now seeing great returns--and so can you.

~ Danny Lyon, area franchisee, The UPS Store,
author of *The Color of My Underwear is Blue*

ANYTHING WITH TWO HEADS IS A FREAK

How to Make Business Partnerships Work:
Why Two People Never Make One Decision

ANYTHING WITH TWO HEADS IS A FREAK

How to Make Business Partnerships Work:
Why Two People Never Make One Decision

DAN RODRIGUEZ
MANON RODRIGUEZ

LIFESUCCESS PUBLISHING, LLC
8900 E Pinnacle Peak Road, Suite D240
Scottsdale, AZ 85255

Telephone:	800.473.7134
Fax:	480.661.1014
E-mail:	admin@lifesuccesspublishing.com
ISBN:	978-1-59930-318-5
Cover :	Daniela A. Savone, LifeSuccess Publishing, LLC
Layout:	Daniela A. Savone, LifeSuccess Publishing, LLC

COMPANIES, ORGANIZATIONS, INSTITUTIONS, AND INDUSTRY PUBLICATIONS: Quantity discounts are available on bulk purchases of this book for reselling, educational purposes, subscription incentives, gifts, sponsorship, or fundraising. Special books or book excerpts can also be created to fit specific needs such as private labeling with your logo on the cover and a message from a VIP printed inside. For more information, please contact our Special Sales Department at LifeSuccess Publishing, LLC.

PROFESSIONAL DISCLAIMER
This book is designed to provide accurate and authoritative information in regard to the subject matter covered and is sold with the understanding that the publisher and author are not engaged in rendering legal, accounting, or other professional service.
If you require legal advice or other professional assistance, the services of a licensed professional in that field should be sought.

With respect to the information contained in the book, the author, editing staff, publisher and any other parties involved in the creation, production, or delivery of this book, are not liable for any direct, incidental, consequential, indirect or punitive damages arising out of your access to, or use of this book.

The author is providing this book and its contents on an "as is" basis and makes no warranty of any kind with respect to this book and its contents. All trademarks are the property of their respective companies.

Likewise, the author disclaims any legal liability of responsibility for the accuracy, completeness, or usefulness of any information, suggestions, formulae, advice, product, or process identified in this book. In addition, the author assumes no responsibility for loss or damages resulting from the use of the information contained in this book.

Dedicated to those who dream big and allow others to partner in that vision.

Acknowledgments

Thanks to our family, friends, and business associates for the inspiration and contribution they've made to this work. Without the partnership and support of others, this book would never have seen a day of light.

We want to express our gratitude to PSI Seminars for showing us how to tap into our personal power and get this book out of our brains and onto paper. Without the encouragement and support of this incredible seminar company, this book would not have been conceived. Thank you Jane C. Willhite, Shirley Hunt, Kathy Quinlan-Perez, Theresa Corbitt, and the entire PSI Seminar family. You're the best!

A debt of gratitude is also owed to Robert G. Allen and the Enlightened Wealth Institute, Stephen Covey and the 7-Habits course, and Senn Delaney's leadership training workshop. We're fortunate to have been taught by the best, so don't be surprised if you recognize bits and pieces of their systems interwoven with our philosophies.

We are also students of books. There are dozens of books published on the topic of business partnerships, and over the years we've read and studied many of them. We acknowledge five partnership books that have had the most influence in the way we create and maintain business partnerships: *Couples at Work* by E. W. "Dub" and Janet James, *Entrepreneurial Couples* by Kathy Marshack, *Forming a Partnership* by Ira Nottonson, *Sleeping with Your Business Partner* by Becky L. Stewart-Gross and Michael J. Gross, and *The Key Questions for Business Partners* by Nina L. Kaufman.

Additionally, we would like to thank the companies and organizations that we have been closely associated with over the years. They have given us the opportunity to sharpen our business partnership skills and become experts in the field. These great institutions include McDonald's Restaurants, Martinizing Dry Cleaning, Society of American Magicians, American Cancer Society, and Rotary International.

A special thanks to Bob Proctor, Gerry Robert, and everyone at LifeSuccess Publishing. We are fortunate to have this great company as our publisher, partner, and teacher. LifeSuccess Publishing held our hands and guided us through the entire authoring process.

With sincere gratitude,

Dan & Manon Rodriguez

CONTENTS

Foreword

Congratulations!

You are in possession of an exceptional book that is required reading for every entrepreneur, manager, and anyone considering starting their first business. It is a complete manual on how to make business partnerships work.

The authors have done an excellent job detailing the ins-and-outs and the ups-and-downs of developing and maintaining effective business relationships. The many tools and techniques described in this book will save you time, money, and frustration. Dan and Manon Rodriguez are not writing from an academic or theoretical point of view. It is evident they live what they write.

The key to unlocking one of the great mysteries of business success is the business partnerships you create. This book is a treasure chest of gold nuggets. It is full of valuable information that can move your business forward and put money in your pocket.

Read it, apply the gold nuggets, and enjoy the success!

- Bob Proctor, bestselling author of
You Were Born Rich* and star of *The Secret

"When you come to a fork in the road ... Take it."

~ Yogi Berra

CHAPTER ONE

Butting Heads for Fun and Profit: The Business Partnership Dilemma

America's economy is based on small businesses. According to a report by the U.S. Small Business Administration (SBA), small businesses are defined as independent businesses having fewer than five hundred employees. The SBA has found that small businesses:

- Represent 99.7 percent of all employer firms
- Employ about half of all private sector employees
- Pay more than 45 percent of total U.S. private payroll
- Have generated 60–80 percent of net new jobs annually over the last decade
- Create more than half of nonfarm gross domestic product (GDP)

Additionally, small innovative firms produce 13 times more patents per employee than large patenting firms, indicating greater creativity among small businesses. The report goes on to say that there are more than *twenty-six million* small businesses in America.

Clearly there is something going on with small business in America. Always considered a land of opportunity, America has been the breeding ground for ambitious men and women for more than 200 years, and never more than today. Every day more entrepreneurs go into business for themselves. Some businesses succeed while others fall by the wayside, but the climate for starting a business has never been better.

Actually, every economic climate is great for starting a business. Whenever there is a weakness in the economy, there is a place for someone with creativity, a good idea, and the courage and resources to start a business. A real entrepreneur always looks for an opportunity. They sell sunglasses when it's sunny and umbrellas when it rains. An entrepreneur finds a need and fills it.

Taking the Plunge ... and the Responsibility

It's relatively easy to start a business. If you have a hobby that you enjoy, you could turn it into a business. Flea markets are full of people who enjoy making crafts—handmade pottery and jewelry, for instance—and who have turned their hobby into a money-making venture. If you collect coins, comic books, or baseball cards, you could turn your collecting hobby into a sales business.

You may have a skill or knowledge that you picked up on your job or over the course of your life. These skills can be turned into a service business that you run either part- or full-time. Your service might provide something that everyone needs—lawn care or a mobile car wash, for example—which requires a lot of work but not a lot of highly technical training. On the other hand, your skill might be something unique that very few people are capable of performing. In either case, you can start a business.

Essentially, anyone can hang out a shingle and start his own business. If you have the courage and the desire, you can start your own business in a very short period of time. Thousands of people have become wealthy and more satisfied with their careers by going into business for themselves.

There are a number of requirements to starting your own business, of course. Many occupations require licensing and certification in order to operate. You may have a great interest in healing, for example, but you can't legally practice medicine without a license. Restaurants and other food services usually require health inspections and other permits.

Will your business require you to buy equipment? If so, can you pay for it out of your pocket or will you have to arrange financing? Financing is a major concern for most small businesses. Uncertainty about how much capital is required to get the business started and keep it going until it is profitable stops many people from pursuing their business ambitions.

If you're selling a product or providing a service, you'll need to get your supplies from somewhere. Will you need to arrange for suppliers? Are there suppliers nearby so you can receive what you need quickly, or will there be a delay because of distance? Will they let you buy on credit, or will they insist on cash? (Financing, once again.)

If you're smart, you'll create a business plan of some sort before you jump into business. Is there a market for what you offer? It used to be that business owners in small towns had a very limited market. Today, with the popularity of the internet, many small business owners have found an enormous market, often over the entire world. You'll want to have an idea of your market to see if your business idea is viable.

To help you make some of these decisions, there are several organizations designed to assist small business owners. The Small Business Administration (SBA) is a government agency that provides support to small businesses. The SBA has publications, classes, and workshops to help potential business owners with subjects such as creating a business plan, learning about technology, financing and accounting, marketing and advertising, and even planning your retirement. Visit SBA's website at www.SBA.gov.

The National Association for the Self-Employed (NASE) is another organization that provides products and resources for its members. The aim of NASE is "to help the self-employed successfully meet the challenges of managing and growing their businesses." The NASE provides support, benefits, and consolidated buying power that have traditionally been available only to larger companies. For more information visit www.NASE.org.

Additionally, many local, state, and federal agencies offer grants, loans, and tax incentives to encourage and help small businesses. American government agencies are interested in supporting small business in many ways. They understand the positive benefit that small businesses provide both to the economy and to citizens' well-being.

Of course, just because it's easy to *start* a business does not mean it's easy to *run* your own business. There is much more to owning your own business than opening the doors and watching money pour in. The startup or acquisition of your own business is an awesome responsibility.

First there is the responsibility that you will assume over the lives, lifestyles, and livelihoods of many people. Your own family will be affected by the amount of time, energy, and resources that you dedicate to the business. You may have to miss out on activities with children or spend money on business activities rather than on the family.

If you have to hire employees, they will be counting on you to provide paychecks to help them support their families and their lifestyles. They will enter into contracts, take out loans, and make financial commitments based on their confidence in you. They may buy a house or a car because they have a job with your company.

Suppliers will devote resources to helping your business. Salespeople will call on you, trucks will deliver supplies to you, and employees of *their* companies will work to assimilate your account into their business. Dozens, even hundreds of people will working to make your business successful.

Then of course there are your customers. Depending on the type of business you start, you could have dozens, hundreds, or thousands of people who alter their routines to frequent your business. They will devote money and energy to your benefit as they trust you with their business. They count on you to provide the product or service that you promised when you sought their patronage.

So if your business fails, you are not the only one who suffers. An entire support structure made of real people will suffer along with you. By starting your business, you take on the responsibility of providing for each of them in some way. Just as you depend on each of them for their individual contribution, they each depend on you and have an investment in your success. They have restructured their lives and their obligations for your benefit.

A lot to think about, isn't it? No one should enter into business lightly. Because as easy as it may be to start your own business, it is much more difficult to get out of a business. Each of those people and institutions you deal with while starting and running your business has a string attached to you and your business, and all of them together form a complex web that is difficult to detach yourself from.

The Costs of Quitting

If you ever consider dissolving your business, you must first take into account your financial obligations. If you borrowed money to start your business, then you still owe that money. The bank won't forgive your loan simply because you decided to close the doors. They made the loan expecting to be paid back—bankers have *their* families and employees to consider as well.

Speaking of employees, yours will have to be paid what you owe them. If payday is next Monday and you decide to close the business on Saturday, then you are still responsible for paying them. Likewise, vendors, utilities, and other bills are still yours to pay. You have a financial obligation to each of these entities.

There are also the legal aspects. To start your own business you may have to enter into a number of contracts—a lease on a building, for example. If you have partners, investors, or other shareholders, there will certainly be legal paperwork involved. To dissolve a business you will have to take action resolve any legal commitments you created. Lawyers will most certainly be involved in this aspect of getting out of business.

Getting out of business is also complicated by the personal relationships that you will have developed. Any business is based to a degree on personal relationships. There is the relationship you developed with your customers or clients: they depended on you for your product or service. There are also the relationships you developed with your employees, if your business required them. After working side by side with someone for hours at a time, it is normal to develop some sort of relationship. This can cause issues of separating personal friendship from business decisions, and some entrepreneurs find themselves trying to keep the business afloat much longer that they should due to these relationships.

As much as we'd like to think we can be completely self-sufficient and independent—the reason many of us start our own business in the first place—the truth is that we depend on other people and they depend on us. You have a moral and ethical obligation to consider your relationships with other people when you decide to end the business you started.

With a partnership, the challenge to get out of business is multiplied. Just as you have financial, legal, and personal obligations to the people who surround you, so does your partner. If you have more than one partner, the concerns increase exponentially. While having partners can spread responsibility for certain tasks, it also complicates matters.

Even the decision itself to get out of business can be more traumatic because partners have input. The business may be the only source of income for a partner, or they may have other reasons that they want to keep the business going. Their reasons to keep the business running may be just as valid as your wish to close it.

Critical Questions to Ask

Because of the complications that can arise should things go wrong, certain questions must be asked and answered honestly before you start your business. It's always tempting to try to just jump in without doing proper preparation, but if you will take the time to answer the following critical questions, your business and partnerships will stand a much better chance of surviving and thriving.

Critical Question #1: Do I really want to own a business? This is the biggest question you can ask yourself. When you answer this question honestly and completely, you have an insight to various aspects of your business—what type of business to own, how involved you want to be, and even what type of customer base you want to have. While there is no right or wrong answer to this question, you can avoid wrong turns in your career and disappointment in your business if you consider your answers when you decide what type of business to start.

For example, your answer to the question may be *I want to be my own boss.* This is a completely valid answer, and probably the number one reason people start their own businesses. They have usually worked for other people who created an environment that may have been unpleasant or simply offended their professional tastes. How many of us have worked in a company and thought, "If they would only do it my way ... ?"

Many businesses have been started because an employee began thinking like an entrepreneur. While working for a company, he saw how it handled its business and became aware of a gap or weakness. In other words, there was an *opportunity.* The gap may have originated from something as simple as geography: a particular neighborhood, area, or region was not served, so the entrepreneur split off to satisfy the demand of that market.

You may also desire the satisfaction of setting your own hours or working from home. Many business owners started their business with this in mind, often because they had small children at home that they had to take care of while making a living. With the fluctuating cost of gasoline, the decision to work out of the house offers a more cost-effective use of resources.

Sometimes the reason behind a person's desire to work at home is more dramatic. Celebrity television chef Paula Deen began her catering business at the age of forty-two, after going through a divorce. Her catering business, "The Bag Lady," delivered bag lunches to customers around the Georgia town where she lived.

Rather than making the deliveries herself, she had her sons do it. Paula suffered from a severe case of agoraphobia—anxiety around people—apparently as a result of having once been robbed at gunpoint while working as a bank teller. The success of "The Bag Lady" led to the opening of her own restaurant, where constant exposure to customers resolved her agoraphobia. Now millions of people know Paula Deen as the outgoing star of cooking shows and the lovable everywoman who inspires others with her story. Her desire to work at home was based on need and a crippling condition. Her drive and desire for success brought her out into the spotlight.

Some people want to start their own business because they have an interest or hobby that absorbs them. Golfers have opened pro shops and become golf instructors, coin collectors have opened coin shops, and chefs like Paula Deen have opened catering businesses—all as a result of their interest in a particular activity.

The move to start your own business often makes very good sense. If you're interested in a subject, then you have likely done a lot of research on the topic, and you know the market and the value of the product or service that you're interested in. What's more, your passion for the subject makes the work environment more pleasant than if you took a random job simply for the paycheck.

Your desire to be your own boss may stem from a need or a mission. You may feel so strongly about a particular product or service that you are compelled to start a business to spread your mission. For example, you may have strong feelings about the environment and, having discovered a great new product that will help keep the environment cleaner or safer, you decide to open a storefront and begin selling the product.

Many people develop a sense of mission about their products. Their passion about what they do or sell can be the key factor in the success of the business. They cannot see themselves working for someone else in a mundane position when there is so much to be accomplished in another occupation.

In a less dramatic fashion, you may want to go into business for yourself because you believe that's the best way to get rich. The desire to make money is a sound one, and it can direct you to make business decisions in a more pragmatic way than some of the other reasons. A healthy respect for money is often the difference between a business that goes under and a business that thrives.

It should be noted that making money and wanting to do good for society are not mutually exclusive. A business can be both profitable and a good corporate citizen. It's important to remember, however, that a business that is closed is no longer in a position to perform good works. As the saying goes, "No margin, no mission."

Critical Question #2: Do I need a partner? Deciding not to "go it alone" is a big step, and the decision can be either a wise one or a foolish one, depending on the circumstances surrounding the partnership. Your answer to this question is the key to your final decision.

You may decide that you want a partner to bolster a relationship. There are many, many businesses that were started by high school or college friends who wanted to work together. Some of these have been great successes. Ben Cohen and Jerry Greenfield met in their seventh grade gym class. Several years later they completed a correspondence course in ice cream making and a year later opened their first ice cream shop in an old gas station.

Today, of course, everyone in America is familiar with Ben and Jerry's ice cream. The two friends combined their quirky personalities with a desire for a high-quality product and marketed it to the public with great success. It probably doesn't matter what type of business they went into; they wanted to work together for the fellowship and fun, and it worked out well for them.

On the other end of the spectrum, you may want partners so they can help finance the operation. Some businesses—restaurants, for example—have high startup costs because of the need for equipment and a building. These costs can run into hundreds of thousands of dollars, or even more. While this is too much money for many people to come up with, partnerships are based on this very principle—split the costs among partners.

In cases like this, some partners may be only marginally acquainted with other partners. Their purpose is to provide funds for the business, and their goal is to achieve a high return on their investment. Although partners should have cordial relations with one another, it is not necessary that they be friends. The partnership is based on business only.

You may want to take on partners because they have a particular areas of expertise. This is common among entrepreneurs who are dynamic at the operations side of a business but may lack the administrative skills to keep the business running smoothly. They will find a partner who can "take care of the paperwork" while they energize investors and employees.

Fairly often a partner is a more experienced businessperson who has the knowledge and resources to help a startup business. If you are starting out in a particular field—for example, buying a franchise—a partner who already knows the industry and business can be very handy. The partner can also serve as a mentor for you while you learn more about how to run the business.

Critical Question #3: Are there other alternatives to having a partner? While taking on partners can certainly be beneficial in many ways, you may have better options. The first choice, of course, is to go it alone. As a sole proprietor you assume all the risk and responsibility … but you also make all the decisions and reap all the rewards.

If you decide you need help, there may be other options. For example, if you need money to start your business, you could seek out investors who are looking for a good return on their investment rather than a piece of the business. At a certain point these investors would be paid off, which is different from taking on financial partners who would retain part ownership of the business.

For financial help, the only limit (legally) is your ingenuity in raising money. Banks and other lending institutions are a resource, but so are private individuals with whom you can arrange loans. Terms, interest rates, payments—these are all determined by how badly you need the money and what the other person is willing to agree to.

If you are looking for expertise, you can consider setting up your own informal "board of advisors"—individuals with whom you can consult on particular questions in their given field. This is where your personality and sales skills come into play. If you can develop a relationship with an expert in a particular area, much (or all) of the advice you get can be had for free.

On the other hand, you may determine that you want to hire someone to advise you in particular areas. Besides the obvious—bookkeepers and lawyers, for instance—think about putting an expert on retainer. If you have a building and equipment, paying someone who is able to repair electrical problems, plumbing, heating, and air conditioning may be a wise investment. If you use a computer, consider putting an expert in computers and software on your payroll.

Critical Question #4: Who is the best partner for me? Sometimes being friends is not enough. Compatibility on a business level is necessary for a partnership to prosper and thrive. When you choose a partner, think about how your personalities will fit, what abilities you each bring to the partnership, and if you share the same vision for the company.

We each carry certain mental programming with us. These are behaviors learned from early childhood that shape our personality. Based on that programming, we have particular traits. Some people are aggressive while others are passive. One person may be empathetic and understanding while another may be cold and aloof.

The blending of personalities in a partnership can work if the chemistry is right between the partners. This is true regardless of whether the partners are alike or opposite in their personalities. Both partners, however, must enter into the partnership feeling respected by the other if the partnership is to be productive.

When you choose a partner, determine if you and the partner can maintain a professional respect for each other. Your styles may differ or be identical regarding particular issues, but unless you have a certain level of regard for the partner, the partnership can suffer. Likewise, you have to consider if the other person has the abilities necessary to be a good partner. Especially if a partner is being sought for a particular area of expertise, that partner must be able to contribute to the partnership. Although a good working relationship is great to have, the relationship will suffer if one partner does not have the abilities necessary to run a business.

What often happens when friends become partners in a business is that one partner will be more capable than the other, creating an imbalance in responsibilities. The capable partner can feel victimized and underappreciated—emotions that are not conducive to a productive partnership. When one partner feels he is carrying more than his share of the load because the other partner doesn't have the ability, resentment soon follows, creating a crisis in the partnership.

Finally, the partner you choose must share the vision that you have for the business. Many businesses have suffered because partners disagreed on which direction the company should go. One might be in favor of rapid expansion and growth, while the other wants more cautious consolidation. Either route might lead to success, but both partners must share the same vision. A conflict between the visions will hurt the business.

Basically the partners must agree on the *why* of the business. Whether it's to make money as quickly as possible, to provide a needed service for the neighborhood, or to improve the world in some small way, agreeing on their motives for starting up a business is crucial. The person you choose must share your vision—or you share theirs—in order for the partnership to function as it should.

Critical Question #5: Do I need a partnership agreement or charter? Understanding beforehand what you expect of each other can prevent problems before they ever occur. Putting that understanding in writing is an excellent way to clarify what each partner's obligations are.

Putting the agreement on paper solidifies the position of each partner. If a partner has doubts about taking on a particular role or responsibility, the act of seeing it on paper can be enough to raise questions. These questions are the ones to answer before forming a partnership, not after everyone is already obligated.

Having a written document also improves everyone's memory. If a question comes up later about a particular function in the partnership, the agreement or charter can be brought out for reference. Without such reference, many failed partnerships have boiled down to one partner saying, "I don't remember agreeing to that."

As a last resort, such a document can be produced in court as evidence of what each partner committed to at the beginning. At this point, of course, the partnership is irrevocably damaged, but just the threat of a document being presented can be enough to keep partners in line with the agreement.

Critical Question #6: Do all partners agree on how to get out of business? As mentioned earlier, getting *out* of a business is much more complicated than getting *into* a business. Whether it's by a vote, by the decision of a single person, or by an objective marker (when a company's losses reach a certain point, for example) the procedure for getting out of business must be spelled out beforehand.

These six critical questions are what every entrepreneur should ask himself before embarking on a startup business. By honestly and thoroughly answering these questions, the possibility for a successful business is multiplied. During the process of answering the questions, the entrepreneur can also learn more about himself and his motivations for going into business.

Partnering with a Friend and Going Broke (Dan)

In 2002, I followed a passion of mine and officially became a Las Vegas show investor and producer. As a part-time professional magician, I had performed in many theatres and stages around the country. However, up to that point I had never worked the showrooms of Las Vegas. Most entertainers have a secret desire to perform in Sin City, and I was no exception.

Performing a magic act, or any act for that matter, in Las Vegas is a rewarding and growing experience, and I learned quickly that the financial risk can outweigh the reward if you don't play your cards right (no pun intended). My plan was not just to get booked to perform my magic act in Las Vegas. My plan was to finance and produce a full-length production show on a major stage and be one of the acts in the show. "Production show" is a trade term that means a show which fills the stage and includes variety acts, dancing showgirls, and anything else that can fit into a one-hour timeslot. Not a cheap venture.

There was no way this project could have succeeded without a partner. I had the money, the desire, and a magic act. What I did not have was the show business experience to put on a production of this magnitude. Only an experienced partner in show business could bring that element into this project.

Paul, a long-time friend, was just the partner. As a singer, dancer, show producer, and director, he had the show production experience and expertise to make this project successful. His strengths were my weaknesses; my strengths were his weaknesses. He brought the music, dance, and theatrical production elements into the show. I brought the money and the vision. We also had very clear roles and responsibilities, we respected each other's decisions, and we shared a common vision. It was a partnership made in heaven.

Paul and I had a successful business partnership that lasted nearly five years. We had the opportunity to perform on many of the grand stages of Las Vegas. Our production company employed dozens of dancers and variety artists, and we entertained thousands of tourists. Our passion and our vision had certainly been fulfilled.

That being said, we learned an additional lesson from this partnership experience. The primary goal of any business partnership is to make a profit. Any expenditure, investment, or business decision must not compromise the primary goal. Paul and I did not have clear income and profit goals, so we failed to consider the return on investment prior to making financial decisions. Most of our decisions were based on a philosophy of doing or paying whatever was needed to get the show opened and on the stage. Our primary goal was to perform in Las Vegas; it was not to make a profit.

Even though our partnership fulfilled its goal of performing in Las Vegas, we did not create a business model that could make a profit. Eventually, our business partnership dissolved because the partnership went broke.

"If you cannot get rid of the family skeleton, you may as well make it dance."

~ George Bernard Shaw

CHAPTER TWO

You Can Have Your Cake and Eat It, Too: Partnering with Family

It's natural to want to go into business with your family. Who else in the world do you know better? The idea of starting your own business might have been discussed for years as part of the family conversation. Preparations may have started long in advance, with the luxury of time to work out all the details.

When deciding whether or not to become partners with a family member, there are several factors to consider. With all the obvious benefits, there can also be some detriments, depending on the family and the particular family member you're thinking about partnering with. It's better to ask and answer questions in advance.

One question to ask may surprise you: Exactly who is "family"? The relationship you have with various members will vary, especially in this day of blended families, single parents, and extended relationships. The most common partner adults choose is their spouse. The idea of sharing not only their family life but their business life as well seems noble and appealing.

We'll go into more detail about the possible problems confronting spouse business partners later, but essentially the problems arise from trying to maintain a relationship, run a household, *and* run a business all at the same time. Meticulous planning and preparation, combined with maturity and understanding, are key.

You may want to go into business with your siblings, your parents, or your children. These are all close relationships that normally go back for many years. Such partners have the advantage of knowing intimately the personalities involved.

Once you get beyond the first branch of the family tree, however, the definition of "family" becomes more ambiguous. Blended families—those families who are composed of two single parents who marry, thus creating a new family (think the Brady Bunch)—are more common today than ever before. You may have siblings, parents, or children who you have known for only a short time.

Add to that the possible number of in-laws that can be considered family, especially if one spouse is pressuring the other to bring them into a "family business." Some people also have a large number of cousins, nieces, nephews, aunts, or uncles who may want to be considered "family"—at least when it comes to business.

It pays to examine the benefits of becoming partners with family members. As we mentioned before, you usually have an extensive knowledge of the personality, quirks, strengths, and weaknesses of the members of your family. Any chance of deceiving you by pretending to be something they're not is long past. Familiarity with the other person is a great benefit to the partnership.

Being as familiar with the partner as you are with a family member also makes communication that much easier. You will have common experiences, common assumptions, and common language to draw upon. Messages can often be communicated with a look or a gesture—sometimes more eloquently than if words were used. Most of us also have a natural desire to benefit family members.

We normally go into business with the idea that we will make money. If we can help a family member make money, then all the better. If the partner is a spouse, then the household benefits from the success of the company.

As we mentioned before, there is often long-term planning in place, sometimes for years before the business is even started. It's not uncommon for a business plan to start as a dream 20 years or more in the making, which matures along with the family members who open the business. The length of time Ben and Jerry spent dreaming of their business is unusual among friends, but it's not unusual among family members.

A business in such a case often has a strong foundation because the concept has been discussed many times over meals; at night before going to bed; and in casual, relaxed moments when dreams and creativity are strongest. When two people share a dream for a long time, it is easier to keep the dream alive when rough spots appear in the road.

Because of this shared dream, there is often a substantial emotional commitment on the part of the partners. The venture becomes more than just a business deal; it becomes a way for family members to realize success with the support of one another, a success that is often more rewarding because of its shared nature. Knowing each other's weaknesses, the partners can step in when they are needed without a lot of turmoil ensuing. Their mutual affection makes the job easier.

Along with all the advantages, there are also some disadvantages. First and foremost is the baggage that family members bring with them. The preconceived notions and perceptions that family can bring into a partnership can work to the detriment of the business. Issues that have little to do with the problem at hand, such as unresolved resentment or petty disputes, can bubble up during times of stress. The professional distance that most of us maintain in our normal work lives is often eliminated when we are dealing with family.

There is also the dynamic of family roles and placement to consider. Many people believe that the older sibling should always take priority, even with regards to making decisions unilaterally. Dominant relationships—a parent and "child," for instance—may be translated to the business environment, regardless of the expertise of the individuals involved. Needless to say, such a stance can be destructive to a partnership and a business.

Family members may feel comfortable ignoring assigned roles in a partnership. Even when roles and responsibilities are clearly spelled out, a family member may take an action or commit to an obligation that is not within her purview. Again, this arises out of a too-comfortable relationship with the other partner, one that violates standard business protocol.

Such a casual relationship can often cause disagreements over the direction of the company. Especially when a business has been successful for a while, the wide range of possibilities for the future may be tempting. An agreed-upon startup vision gives way to disunity as each family member/partner has a different opinion on which way to go.

One factor that is sometimes overlooked is the impact that a successful family partnership and business can have on those family members who are *not* part of the business. The success of a few members of the family may lead to jealousy and resentment from the rest of the family. Especially if the business is wildly successful, siblings and other relatives may start to feel left out—even if they were given the opportunity to join in when the business started. Emotions such as these are not always logical or reasonable, but they can be harmful.

While there are no guarantees against problems in a family partnership, there are some tools, techniques, and strategies that can help you to avoid some of them and to minimize the damage done by those that do occur.

Put it in writing. Legal documents and signed paperwork are not absolute safeguards, but they beat having nothing at all. The purpose of having documentation of all agreements, assignments, and responsibilities is not to produce them in a court of law. If a dispute has gotten that far, the damage to the relationship is already done. Rather, documentation is designed to remind partners—even family members—of what they agreed to beforehand.

Family members who want to be partners in a business may object to having to resort to "legal stuff" when partnering with family. They may try to convince you that the family bond is strong enough to handle any disputes. The truth is much different: if it ever comes to the point where documentation would be needed, the family bond has long been forgotten.

With that in mind, **a mission statement or written list of priorities** will clarify matters substantially. Having the written list to refer to can "remind" family members who might have decided to go off course. The desire to go in different directions is sometimes based on differing visions, but it is also often based on petty disputes and temporary emotions. By agreeing to the written priorities, each partner can work through arguments or disagreements in a professional manner.

Written schedules, calendars, and timelines are also good tools to help avoid problems. Family partners especially can be tempted to procrastinate on a project or task, thinking that they will be "forgiven" by the other partner. Time tools are excellent ways to encourage a family member to conduct herself in a professional way and to keep commitments in a timely manner. Projects are sometimes stymied because one partner neglected to complete her part on time.

There are also a few techniques that can help any partnership, but which are especially important when partnering with a family member. **Open communication** is an absolute requirement. By creating written expectations beforehand and communicating effectively, partners can avoid most problems.

Trouble starts when one partner harbors resentment against another for some transgression, imagined or real. With open communication, such resentment is dealt with quickly, before it has a chance to take root. Personal slights, as the result of a misunderstanding, are one of the most common causes of difficulties in a partnership. Talking openly about such emotional matters can head off trouble before it starts.

Being aware of stress levels in yourself and in your partner will also pay dividends. With family members, you can often see the signs of stress before they are aware of it themselves. This is one of the times where your familiarity with your partner really pays off. When you see the signs of stress, communicate with her and find out if there is a problem.

When you ask someone if she is under stress, her first instinct might be to deny it. If that's the case, communicate freely with her; tell her what you observed and offer assistance. Besides being the proper thing to do, offering to help a family partner benefits the partnership, the business, and the relationship. But it doesn't work unless you stay alert for signs of stress.

There are a few strategies that, if you use them, can smooth the way for a successful family partnership. First and foremost**, try to keep family and business matters separate**. This is often difficult, especially when you work with a spouse all day and then go home. Spending so much time together can easily lead to conflicts. The effect of these conflicts can be minimized by trying not to let troubles in one aspect of your life bleed over into other aspects.

While a natural inclination is to carry conversations and problems between home and work (we usually want to solve problems as quickly as possible), there is a time and a place for problem solving, and solving personal problems at work or work problems at home is usually not appropriate. The couple that discusses work at home can soon find themselves not talking about anything else (and vice versa). Consciously try to avoid mixing the two.

Another strategy is to **do your best to maintain a flexible schedule**. While working regular hours and being dependable are important, one of the best aspects of owning your business is that you can make time for your family life. Baseball and soccer games, recitals and school programs, special times with family—these are all more important in the long run than adhering to a concrete work schedule.

There are always times of imbalance, of course, when you will have to work long hours at the business in order to make it successful. It's when these imbalances become the norm that you need to realize what you're missing out on in your personal life. Especially to an ambitious family team, working together to build a business can be very rewarding. However, the business exists to benefit your personal life, not the other way around. Taking control of your schedule and making time for family will make for a better business *and* a happier family.

As mentioned before, when some members of the family are part of the business, other members can feel excluded, which can lead to resentment. A strategy to help you avoid such problems is to **involve other family members in the business**. Finding a way to include the rest of the family both allays jealous feelings and spreads the pride of working in a family-owned business.

It's important that the included family members make actual contributions to the business and don't serve as "token" representatives. They should be held accountable for their responsibilities just as anyone else who works for the company. Besides the possible negative fallout among other employees, and the resulting problems with morale, a family member who actually contributes also enjoys the pride of being part of something bigger than themselves.

If you have determined that you are going to partner with your spouse, then each of you will have particular roles and responsibilities. There are different categories that typically describe the relationship that develops when a couple works together in their own business. These categories are based on how involved both spouses are in the business.

Solo entrepreneur with supportive spouse. Many small businesses fall into this category. Typically one spouse is self-employed while the other spouse is not part of the business. Many service businesses in which the labor and skills are specialized are organized this way (i.e., electricians, plumbers, and consultants).

Many businesses are structured this way, of course, so the option is not limited to service businesses. There may be family obligations that prevent one spouse from being involved in the business. Situations such as having small children or having a family member who needs extensive care can keep one spouse extraordinarily busy while the other runs the business.

In this kind of arrangement, one partner is 100 percent responsible for owning and running all aspects of the business. Key business decisions are made by that one individual, who either benefits or suffers from the decision. The most important decision is what direction the company will go, and this decision rests on the single individual.

The non-business spouse is not completely left out, of course. He may provide part-time help when he can. While decisions affecting the company are made by the one spouse, the other spouse can serve as a sounding board, providing another perspective based on his knowledge of the situation. Many times, this service is the most valuable that he can provide.

Another benefit the non-business spouse often provides is when he works outside the home. Especially when a business is just getting off the ground, cash flow can be a problem for the household. That extra paycheck is often what enables the entrepreneur to keep working at the business until it reaches profitability.

Perhaps the number one thing the non-business spouse can offer is emotional support. Starting a business has many ups and downs, and even the road to a successful business is filled with disappointments. A supportive, sympathetic spouse can be the extra spark that the entrepreneur needs to keep going.

Co-entrepreneurs, also termed *copreneur* ("couple" + "entrepreneur"), was coined by Frank and Sharon Barnett in 1988 to describe couples in which both partners own and manage a joint business together. More than just business partners and more than just partners in life, copreneurs illustrate and exercise the dynamics of balancing love and work.

Changes in society have made copreneurial couples more common. Just a couple decades ago women were homemakers, expected to take care of the household while the husband went out to work. Today more women are finding satisfaction in the workplace, and not necessarily in menial jobs. The ambition to start and grow a business resides in many people, regardless of gender.

At the same time, many people aspire to having a loving family. By sharing their business successes with a spouse, copreneurs have managed to reach for both worlds. The business itself can become one of their "children" as they nurture it and try to encourage its healthy growth.

The trend has become so common that there is even an organization to support copreneurial couples. The National Copreneur Society (www.copreneursociety.org) has as its mission "to strengthen the entrepreneurial couple (copreneur) relationship in life and business."

The benefits to the company are many. If one of the partners is ill, out of town, or simply takes a day off, the other is in place to watch the business and keep it going. By allowing for such absences, the dreaded "burnout" that happens to many entrepreneurs from working too many hours can be avoided.

Also, although I recommended against it earlier, a copreneurial couple *can* have productive business discussions away from the pressure of the company. When they are relaxed and at ease, the partnering couple can often discuss business items in a way that would be impossible during operating hours. They can both be more creative and at the same time more receptive to the other's ideas and opinions. Problems in the business are often solved over dinner or at the breakfast table. One warning, however: although it can be exceedingly useful, when this type of discussion becomes common, it's time to refocus on separating business and personal time.

Dual entrepreneurs. When each of the spouses has his or her own business, completely separate from the other, it is an example of *dual entrepreneurship*. Both partners are self-employed, owning and managing their own business. Although they may provide each other with emotional support, neither has any responsibility toward the other's business.

Many dual entrepreneur couples started out running solo entrepreneurships. With one partner fully engaged in business and all its accompanying excitement (and often its substantial monetary rewards), the other spouse catches the "bug" and wants to become an entrepreneur also. Excitement about "winning big" is often contagious.

The new entrepreneur may feel, however, that he doesn't want to get into the same business, profession, or even industry as the spouse who is already running a business. She may find the possibility of competing with his spouse distasteful or worry about the effect it will have on the family's unity.

Often, then, the new entrepreneur will find another type of business to go into, usually one with completely different challenges, questions, and situations. The idea here is to make the new business as completely separate from the established business as possible. What this does, of course, is set up an entirely new set of rules, schedules, and concerns—ones with which the other, better established spouse is unfamiliar. Although some of the questions at the beginning may be the same, the operation of separate businesses is, beyond a few general principles, a whole new ball game.

Having separate enterprises can be rewarding for both partners as they work at their own businesses to prosper. An entrepreneur can look with pride at any company she has started which then goes on to become larger and more successful. Being part of the process from the very beginning is one of the most rewarding aspects of entrepreneurship.

The dual entrepreneur couple faces many challenges, however. All of the difficulties that the average two-career family faces will be multiplied in the dual entrepreneur family. There may be conflict over the allocation of family resources between the two businesses. (If children are old enough to help, for example, whose business do they help first?) For that matter, there may be conflict over whose business is "more important." One business may generate more income than the other. However, the less remunerative business may offer emotional rewards to the spouse that runs it. On a list of priorities, how are the various "rewards" ranked? Only an in-depth conversations held *in advance* can smooth these situations over.

If a couple has small children, who babysits over the weekend while the other works? Some may automatically (and unfairly) assume that the mother should take care of the children, but that does not give equal validity to the businesses at all. When the partners have family responsibilities, accommodations at the business will have to be set up so that one of the partners can take time off to care for the children.

Travel and work schedules will also need to be coordinated. Couples must set aside resources to handle extra expenses such as last-minute babysitters or airline ticket purchases (which are often cheaper when bought in advance). Emergencies and last-minute urgencies happen all the time in a small business, and the conflict between spouses that may result can cause mayhem in a household. Advance planning can avoid many of these pitfalls, but invariably something will happen that the couple did not prepare for. Setting priorities that both spouses agree to can make the decisions easier when problems arise.

The demands of two independent businesses can also subtract from the quantity and quality of "together" time for a couple. A business owner's scheduled work time may be limited, but the responsibility for the business is 24/7. When you have two sets of employees, two sets of vendors, two sets of customers, two sets of *everything*—it's extremely difficult to make time for the family and other relationships.

The bottom line on all of these scenarios is that the entrepreneurial life is difficult for couples, but it can also be very rewarding. Advance planning and open communication can help entrepreneurial couples avoid many potential problems, but even more is needed. Each of the partners, whether working together or working separately, must exhibit a high level of commitment to the relationship as well as to the business(es). The partners must also be mature enough to handle the inconveniences and occasional lapses in understanding that can happen with a busy entrepreneur. An independent spirit and a well-developed sense of empathy will go a long way toward making the entrepreneurial relationship a successful and happy one.

Partnerships Don't Have Two Heads (Manon)

From the early 1980s through the mid 1990s, Dan and I worked for an advertising agency that represented McDonald's Restaurants. We traveled the western half of the United States visiting hundreds of McDonald's restaurants each year. Our job was to consult with McDonald's owners/operators about implementing a media and marketing plan for their restaurant. Not only did we assist them in their media and marketing plan, we also developed many strong friendships over the fifteen years we were employed by the advertising agency.

Over time, these successful individuals became our role models, and we wanted to become McDonald's owners like them. During our many restaurant visits we took every opportunity to spend as much time as possible with each owner/operator. We often went out to dinner, performed extra duties, and stayed extra days. Every opportunity we had, we asked them to share their ideas for succeeding in the restaurant business. They knew that our dream was to become McDonald's owners, and they were always willing to share. These successful entrepreneurs spent hours telling us about the pitfalls and glories of the business. They shared paperwork procedures, charts, worksheets, and vendor contacts that would make our lives easier. We acquired an incredible arsenal of tools to help us become successful McDonald's owners/operators.

These experiences taught us that successful people often want to share their wisdom and are honored when asked for advice. One owner/operator team had words of wisdom for us that we follow to this day. Those words of wisdom became one of the core principles of our success. In fact, one of these maxims became the title of this book.

This particular owner/operator team consisted of a husband and wife. They were copreneurs and were both actively involved in their restaurant business. The restaurant was definitely operating as a well-oiled machine. We observed how well the employees and owners communicated with each other. We asked many questions, including how they were able to successfully work the same business that was open seven days a week, eighteen hours a day. How did they keep stress and frustration from affecting their relationship? The husband explained to us that there was only one way to work a partnership. "I have my jobs and responsibilities, and she has hers. I don't interfere with her job, and she does the same for me. Our employees like it that way. They know who to talk to when an issue comes up. After all, anything with two heads is a freak."

"Doing nothing is very hard to do ... you never know when you're finished."

~ Leslie Nielsen

CHAPTER THREE

Where's the Beef?: Partnering with Business and Industry

The Merriam-Webster dictionary definition of *partnership* is "a team of two or more people who own or operate a business." While technically correct, that definition is unnecessarily limiting, and in today's business world a more expansive definition will work better for the entrepreneur looking to start and run a successful business.

The best working definition of a "partner" is to think of a person as a "stakeholder." A stakeholder is someone who has a vested interest —a "stake"— in the well-being of you and of your business. This may include the people who are part owners or operators of your business, as in the definition above, but the circle extends far beyond the narrow walls of your business.

With the new definition in mind, you can see that you have the ability to turn almost anyone into a partner or a stakeholder. If you walked up to a stranger on the street and said "I will give you half of all the profits that my company makes," then you would have just created a stakeholder. That person would suddenly develop an *intense* interest in the success and profitability of your business!

If that technique would work on a stranger (far-fetched though the example is), then what if you could do something similar with those people, companies, organizations, etc. that you actually have contact with? What if you could turn your entire community into a stakeholder, a partner, interested in your business's success?

How could you do such a thing? How would you make someone a stakeholder? The example above was an extreme example of the technique of **sharing profits**. Too much of that kind of example would make the business unprofitable, of course. But what if you partnered with someone who could give you more business, thus increasing your profit? Would you be willing to share some of the increase in profits with that partner?

Many businesses do just that, partnering with organizations to conduct such charitable events as car washes. The heightened visibility of the company, thanks to the advertising and appeal of a charity car wash, increases business that day. As a result, many businesses agree to donate a certain amount of their increase in business that day to the charity. The business has made that charity a *stakeholder*.

By the same token, you and a partner business might agree to **share business**. If the two businesses share the same target market, one might sell one product to the customer while the other business sells a different, noncompeting product. Most malls work on a variation of this principle, with the different businesses in the mall selling products to the same target customers. Another example is the trend of bookstores to install a coffee shop inside their building. The coffee shop gets the extra business by providing customers a place to relax with a drink and a snack while browsing through a book or magazine. The bookstore gets extra business because the customers spend more time in the store, which normally equates to increased sales.

Besides sharing business, two partnering businesses might **share customers**. This is a bit different, as it might be as simple as each business directing their customers to the other business. For example, a store that sells kitchen knives might give each customer a business card for a person who operates a knife-sharpening service. That person, in turn, may recommend the brand of knives sold in that store.

As you can tell by these examples, the ability to partner with someone else is limited only by your imagination. Creativity and flexibility, along with knowing your market and customer base, can provide you with opportunities to increase your business by helping others increase theirs.

Types of Partnerships

What types of partnerships are available? If you think of every interaction you have as a business interaction, then you can see why everybody you speak with is a potential partner. In fact, you might consider your *relationships* as partnerships. Here are a few examples of different types of partnerships or relationships.

Franchisor–franchisee. One of the most popular ways of starting your own business today is through *franchising*. What is franchising? It can be the licensing of a trademark or a way of doing business, such as Martinizing Dry Cleaning, which involves a particular method and high standard of quality for cleaning clothes.

The franchise can also give you "permission" to buy into and run a business, based on an established business model, such as McDonald's restaurants. Many entrepreneurs have made their fortunes by becoming franchisees of some of the most recognized brand names in America today. The parent company, the *franchisor*, benefits as well as the entrepreneur, the *franchisee*.

When we speak of franchises, the word is often used in different ways. The media often uses the term *franchise* to describe ownership of the characters and/or setting of a film, video game, or book (for example, the "Batman franchise" or the "Star Wars franchise"). While these examples are certainly money-makers, they are not usually within the reach of most entrepreneurs wanting to start a business.

Franchise also refers to the exclusive right to sell a particular product, or brand of product or merchandise. The websites of manufacturers will often provide a list of "authorized dealers" for their products within a certain area. The name recognition of the merchandise is such that the manufacturer has decided, for whatever reason, to limit distribution of its product to certain individuals or companies.

Often more useful for the entrepreneur is the definition of franchise most people use: when a retail company, often a chain, shares its brand and central management with individuals who pay the company for the privilege. The entrepreneur usually pays an up-front amount to the company and usually an ongoing fee, often called the "franchise fee" or "royalty fee."

There may also be a deposit required, so the company can research the territory or market, as well as an advertising fee, so the parent company can effectively advertise in the market. The potential franchisee needs to ask questions about ongoing fees well before agreeing to purchase the franchise. For example, how much is the royalty fee? How often is it to be paid? Is it a percentage, a fixed amount, or a combination? If it's a percentage, what is it based on? Finally, how does this percentage and fee situation compare to other comparable franchises?

Many of the initial fees go to cover expenses incurred by the parent company in research, equipment, stationery, recruitment, training, and franchise launch. Most franchisors provide a high level of support to franchisees so that they can maintain the integrity and consistency of the brand. While the franchisee has concerns about the profit that he will make from the business, the franchisor is concerned with the effect the new business will have on its established businesses.

The potential for franchises is nearly unlimited. Depending on the entrepreneur's particular interests and financial situation, companies are franchising more than ever, providing opportunities for thousands of ambitious people to start their own business.

For example, here is a list of the top ten franchise opportunities for 2008, as chosen by Entrepreneur.com:

1. Subway
2. McDonald's
3. Liberty Tax Service
4. Sonic Drive In Restaurants
5. InterContinental Hotels Group
6. Ace Hardware Corp
7. Pizza Hut
8. UPS Store
9. Circle K
10. Papa John's Int'l, Inc.

For those who are looking for home-based franchises, here is Entrepreneur.com's top ten list for 2008:

1. Jani-King
2. Jan-Pro Franchising Int'l, Inc.
3. Servpro
4. ServiceMaster Clean
5. Snap-on Tools
6. Stratus Building Solutions
7. Matco Tools
8. Jazzercise, Inc.
9. Vandguard Cleaning Systems
10. Bonus Building Care

These "top ten" lists are different from the ones for previous years and will be different from the years that follow. These simply show the variety of opportunities that are available to entrepreneurs. Besides the ones listed, there are hundreds of other franchises, some of which are just beginning to become popular. The next "hot" franchise will be the company that provides a product or service that the public demands, and the public's tastes change quickly.

A franchise can benefit the entrepreneur in many ways. First, of course, is name recognition. When the average person hears the name McDonald's or Pizza Hut, for example, they know exactly what they are going to get. They form an image in their mind of the building, the products and the service that they can expect. An established brand has a built-in clientele.

The franchisee benefits from the name recognition by not having to spend money on introducing the business to customers. Advertising dollars can be spent in other ways, and marketing can focus on other, more profitable, areas. Rather than worry about how to get customers, the franchisee can concentrate on providing superior service and quality to the existing customer base.

A franchisee also benefits from the company's established procedures. Depending on the organization, these can cover everything from the product itself to hiring and training employees to advertising to customer relations. Some companies are more thorough and demanding than others and insist that proper policies and procedures be followed for every detail. Others are looser with their requirements, allowing franchisees a certain amount of freedom and autonomy.

The owner of a single startup restaurant, for example, might spend an extraordinary amount of time and energy developing the proper menu. He would have to take into consideration the tastes of his customer base, the amount of preparation necessary, his ability to get supplies in a timely manner, and many other variables.

By purchasing a franchise from an existing restaurant chain—KFC or McDonald's, for example—the menu is already figured out, and suppliers are already arranged. The brand name automatically appeals to a certain segment of the population. So having an existing menu package as part of the franchise alleviates much of the stress the restaurateur might face.

Marketing support is another benefit a franchise can deliver. Larger companies purchase time on network television—something beyond the ability of most single businesses to afford. The franchises each pay into an advertising account, and the money that they contribute is pooled so as to purchase larger media packages, resulting in much more exposure. The advertising spots that the company buys have a larger impact than what the individual contributors could purchase on their own.

Some companies spend a larger share of their budget on advertising than do others. Companies such as McDonald's are heavily involved in advertising and thus have a higher profile than some other businesses. This higher profile can influence the customer base more effectively, increasing business at each of the stores. The individual franchisee may not need to do as much local advertising, thus increasing profitability.

Franchisees get the benefit of the power of numbers. Most companies that franchise have a system in place so that their franchisees can get better prices on supplies than they might be able to negotiate for themselves. Each franchisee gets the buying power of a much larger company. This helps the businesses get specialty products along with lower prices.

There are, of course, some drawbacks to franchising (or what some people might consider to be drawbacks). First of all you must share your profits with the larger company, in the form of royalties, advertising fees, and other fees and charges. While you get the benefit of better advertising and marketing, these are more useful in some markets than in others. Those fees come right out of your profits.

You also lose a measure of independence when you franchise rather than start your own business. Those policies and procedures that the parent company hands down can feel restrictive to some people, especially independent entrepreneurs who want to be their own boss. The entrepreneur may have an idea that they think will be better suited for their own store, yet they may be prevented from implementing it by the restrictions the company imposes. Most companies that franchise have a system in place where a franchisee can make suggestions about a new product or procedure, but the company has the final say regarding the business. Particularly to the person who goes into business to be their own boss, the "final say" may be too much for them to take.

Some people are tinkerers. They love to make small changes and adjustments to different parts of their lives to search for improvements. For those people, experimentation is a way of life and is part of what makes their world and environment bearable. Having the world stay the same all the time is difficult for them. Needless to say, companies don't universally approve experimentation from their franchisees. Although they try to give franchisees some freedom, the company's franchise system depends on central control to be able to maintain the company brand. Quality control is uppermost for the company, and although the franchisee might provide excellent quality, the company does not want its product or service diluted unnecessarily.

For franchisees, there is always the chance that the company will go in a direction they don't like. If the company develops and promotes a new product or service, it will expect all of its stores to follow suit. Regardless of the franchisee's feelings, he will have to do what the company says. For example, a company may decide to promote a particular cause or convey a particular message that the individual franchisee disagrees with. The company may do an infinite number of things that the franchisee, the entrepreneur, does not want to do. If the company continues in a certain direction, the franchisee may find himself faced with a choice between owning a franchise that he no longer supports or selling out.

Obviously there are a lot of problems that can crop up in the franchisor–franchisee relationship. Most problems, however, are not new and have been faced and solved before. The challenge is to find the resources you need so as to be able to solve your problems in the most efficient and effective way possible.

Here are a few resources available to the franchisee:

- International Franchise Association (IFA)

  1501 K Street NW Suite 350

  Washington DC 20005

  Phone: (202) 628-8000

  Website: www.franchise.org

  This association is open to members. It is an organization of franchisees, franchisors, and suppliers. Their website is "dedicated to providing … members and guests with a one-stop shopping experience for franchise information."

- Franchise Times Magazine

  Website: www.franchisetimes.com

  "The news and information source for franchising," Franchise Times offers many different pieces of information on franchising, including information on books, conferences, directories, and guides for anyone interested in franchising.

- New England Franchise Association (NEFA)

  125 Church Street

  PMB 90-344

  Pembroke MA 02359

  Phone: (617) 469-3002

  Website: www.nefranchise.org

The NEFA is an association of franchisors, franchisees, and suppliers "promoting the responsible growth of franchising throughout New England by fostering positive communication, learning and best practices."

- American Association of Franchisees and Dealers (AAFD)

  PO Box 81887

  San Diego CA 92138-1887

  Phone: (800) 733-9858

  Website: www.aafd.org

  "The AAFD is a national non-profit trade association dedicated to defining and promoting Total Quality Franchising practices."

- American Franchisee Association (AFA)

  53 West Jackson Boulevard, Suite 1157

  Chicago IL 60504

  Phone: (312) 431-1469

  Website: www.franchisee.org

  The AFA is a "national trade association of franchisees and dealers [which] works to improve the industry of franchising while protecting its members' economic investments in their businesses."

Vendor/supplier. When you think of creating partnerships based on relationships, one of the most rewarding of these is the partnership you develop with vendors. In most businesses, suppliers have the biggest impact on profitability and the smooth operation of the business. Without supplies, you either have no product to sell or you don't have the products you need to perform your service. Establishing a productive relationship with your suppliers helps ensure the success of your company.

Besides conducting normal transactions, how do you effectively partner with a vendor? One way is for you to remain brand loyal. In other words, you buy all the products you need from the one vendor, or at least all the products that they offer that you use. When you do that, the vendor recognizes that he can depend on your business and develop stability of his own; he gets more sales and profits from your loyalty. The vendor, on the other hand, must assure you of several things in return for your loyalty. First, the products you need must always be in stock. Few things hurt a small business more than not being able to conduct that business due to lack of supplies. The vendor can take this particular burden off of you.

The vendor can also ensure good service and the best price available. Everyone wants top service and the lowest price, but in this case you have made a commitment to a vendor who, in a true partnership based on relationships, has added motivation to offer you the best service and price he can manage.

You might also feature that vendor's products in your marketing. There are often marketing arrangements between vendor and business where they both benefit from the marketing of particular products. The vendor gets his product featured, and you get the brand recognition and sometimes added funds to help with your marketing. Brand recognition is often a big benefit to the small business owner. Those who purchase franchises already enjoy this benefit, but the entrepreneur who is starting from scratch looks for every edge he can get. If he purchases a name brand product from his supplier and features it in marketing, it adds credibility to his business.

By partnering with a vendor, the business also enjoys consistency in its products, in service, and in quality. A business whose quality and service are inconsistent has trouble developing customer loyalty. One of the advantages of large brand names such as McDonald's is that customers know what to expect. Because McDonald's closely monitors its supply channel, each restaurant enjoys standardization and consistency that is not available to nonbranded restaurants.

The vendor can enjoy benefits from the partnership other than increased sales. Eventually the supplier can develop more efficiency in supplying what the business needs, which translates to increased profits. As the small business grows, the supplier enjoys increased business also. Working with small businesses in such a way creates a good reputation in the community, which adds to the vendor's success.

We may not consciously recognize it, but we see partnering between businesses and vendors all the time. A supermarket may have special displays featuring a particular brand and item. A restaurant may display a sign signifying that it proudly serves a certain brand of coffee. Vendors and businesses work together to promote both their businesses.

Customers. You may believe that your relationship with your customers ends after the transaction is finished. Nothing could be further from the truth. When done properly, the partnership between a business and its customers is the most important factor in that business's success. To be sure, your business can simply run on "transactions." But why would you settle for that when you can build your business by making your customers partners—that is, by making them stakeholders?

How do you go about involving the customers in your business so that they have a stake in its well-being? First, you have to produce a product or service that your customers need. *Need*, in this case, is anything that makes your customers' lives easier, more convenient, or just plain *better*. Any product or service can meet this definition as long as it is provided in a competent, professional manner.

This first step in your relationship with your customers is important. If you consistently provide the best service you are capable of, your customers will recognize this and frequent your business. Moreover, they will tell others about your business. One rule of thumb is that a satisfied customer tells three people about their experience, while a dissatisfied customer tells ten people. Word of mouth can build your business without you having to spend a penny on advertising.

Basically, you want to make your customers happy that they do business with you. Regardless of what business you are in, satisfied customers are your ultimate product. They will build your business for you. They instinctively understand the partnership concept, and good customers will help you in ways you may not realize. How can this partnership help you? By increasing business and profits, of course. These are the two most basic goals of any business. But beyond the financial aspect, your customers can make running your business more pleasant for you.

Every business owner knows there are rough spots in running a business. It may be that an employee doesn't show up as scheduled, a supplier is late delivering merchandise that you need, or one of an infinite number of other potential problems occurs. When this happens, it can have an impact on the service you provide your customers.

If you have built a strong partnership with your customers, they will be more understanding when your business hits a rough patch. As long as high-level service is the norm, you can minimize the number of irate customers you encounter, as well as their level of displeasure with you and your business. That kind of relationship takes extraordinary conscientiousness on your part, but remember that your customers are not in the way of your business; they are the reason you are in business.

If you have great communication with your customers, they will often lead you in a direction that adds to your business. Listen to your customers and their suggestions, as they know what they want before you do. For example, a restaurant's customers might announce to the owner that they want a particular kind of pie or a particular brand of soft drink. If he hears the same request enough, the smart business owner will see if he can satisfy that request.

Other partnerships are available to the aware entrepreneur. Service and trade organizations are good places to start. When you join an organization and become involved, you reap the reward. For example, besides enjoying the fellowship you have with others who are in situations similar to yours, you can also pick up tips from them and learn of trends in your industry or in your community.

Let's say that you own an independent restaurant. As a restaurant owner you might join the state and national restaurant associations. These will put you in touch with other restaurant owners who have concerns very similar to yours. You can also find out about new trends that are developing that might benefit your business.

You might also join the local chamber of commerce and become an active and visible member of the community. In this way, you become your own advertising since local concerns often come up at chamber of commerce meetings. Being active in service and trade organizations helps your business by making you more aware and more visible, and it makes owning your own business more pleasant and rewarding.

Other forms of partnering are also possible:

- **Co-branding**: where two or more companies form an alliance to work together to market goods or services
- **Co-op advertising**: where two or more manufacturers or retailers share the cost of advertising a common brand, product, or service
- **Affiliate partners**: where you consciously direct your customers to partner businesses
- **Joint venture partners:** where two separate enterprises partner to share expertise and resources

The important thing is to look at all areas of your life and look to establish partnerships rather than just "do business" or "have a relationship." By working toward making each interaction win-win, you develop partners who will help you and your business become successful.

Are there business models out there that are already doing what you want to do? Find out what it takes to partner with them. The franchisor–franchisee relationship is a perfect example of such a partnership. Partnerships are the key to successful business interactions.

First Big Break in Big Business (Dan)

McDonald's is one of the most difficult franchise businesses to purchase. Of the tens of thousands of applications McDonald's Corporation receives each year from prospective franchisees, fewer than two hundred applicants eventually make it through the hoops and are offered a restaurant.

Manon and I were not discouraged by those statistics, and in 1989 we joined the masses and submitted our franchisee application to purchase a McDonald's Restaurant. Three months of waiting ended when we received a letter from McDonald's Corporation stating that they appreciated our interest in purchasing a McDonald's franchise. The letter went on to explain that as there were more qualified applicants, our application was rejected and we would not be considered to become a McDonald's franchisee.

End of story? Not yet.

We called McDonald's corporate headquarters to get a more detailed explanation as to why our application was rejected. We were not going to accept a simple "thanks, but no thanks" letter and give up our dream of becoming a McDonald's franchisee—at least, not without a fight. The response from the company was short, specific, and discouraging. We did not have enough available cash, our net worth was not sufficient, and we did not have enough business education or business experience.

How do you challenge that? The unfortunate fact was that they were right. We only had $5000 in the bank. We had a home, two cars and loans to go with them, and neither of us had a college degree or extensive business experience.

Instead of becoming discouraged and giving up our dream of becoming a McDonald's franchisee, we committed to persisting and changed our lifestyle. We focused full time on becoming a qualified applicant. We became students of business and took business classes. To save money we sold our home and moved into the basement of my parents' house. On a monthly basis I sent McDonald's Corporation an updated financial statement and a report on our personal development. This went on for over a year, and yet we never heard from McDonald's.

Nearly two years after we submitted our original prospective franchisee application, we got a call from McDonald's Corporation. They informed us that we still did not meet the company's minimum requirements. However, they were so impressed with our persistence and determination that they had agreed to bend the rules and grant us a franchise opportunity. In August of 1994, we became official McDonald's owners/operators.

McDonald's founder, Ray Kroc, would often talk about the importance of persistence and determination in his speeches. He had a favorite quote by Calvin Coolidge that clearly explains why we eventually became McDonald's owners: "Nothing in this world can take the place of persistence. Talent will not; nothing is more commonplace than unsuccessful people with talent. Genius will not; unrewarded genius is almost a proverb. Education will not; the world is full of educated derelicts. Persistence and determination alone are omnipotent."

"The Doc told me I had a dual personality. Then he lays an 82 dollar bill on me, so I give him 41 bucks and say, 'Get the other 41 bucks from the other guy.'"

~ Jerry Lewis

CHAPTER FOUR

Understanding the Nature of the Beast: Defining Entrepreneurial and Behavioral Styles

Each of us is unique. Biologically, our individual characteristics are carried in our chromosomes, each of which harbors various traits—the shape of our chin, our nose, and our ears; whether we'll be tall or short, fat or thin, dark or fair—all of the physical characteristics that make us recognizable.

Our personalities are also part of our genetic makeup, but to complicate matters more, we are also the product of all of the experiences we've ever had. Identical twins come from the same egg, and yet even when they are raised in the same household under almost identical conditions, their personalities can vary wildly.

As adults we have learned to adapt our behavior to the people around us to make working with others easier and more productive. We minimize certain aspects of our personality and emphasize other parts, all for the purpose of cooperating and smoothing the social interactions that we engage in. The people we interact with do the same (if they are interested in making the relationship work).

Almost any personality type can start and run a successful business, as long as the entrepreneur understands her own personality—her strengths and weaknesses—and incorporates techniques that play to her strengths while minimizing her weaknesses. For example, when a right-handed carpenter drives a nail into a board, she doesn't use her left hand. She holds the hammer in the strong hand so she can better perform the job. The decision to use the right hand doesn't make her weak or dependent; rather, she recognizes the aspects of her personality that will help her perform her best, and she focuses on those traits.

In the same way, entrepreneurs who point their strengths at the task at hand are not "compensating" or otherwise using a crutch to do their job. Playing to your strengths is the smart way to do business, and successful entrepreneurs know this. The ancient Greek saying "Know thyself" still applies today. Knowing your own strengths and weaknesses is the first step toward being able to work with others in a productive and positive way.

When you want to partner with someone in a business, the complexity of the relationship demands that you not only know your own strengths and weaknesses but also those of your partner. Additionally, the traits, characteristics, and techniques that your partner uses should also be part of your knowledge. Only by having knowledge of one another can partners form a strong, productive alliance.

When you and your partner know each other well, and when each understands the other's strengths and weaknesses, you can assign roles that will maximize each other's strengths, thus making the partnership more effective. This process takes cooperation and participation by everyone involved. With the contribution of self-knowledge and self-awareness, each partner becomes stronger individually and also makes the partnership stronger.

For the effective leader in today's world, the ability to understand the differences in behavioral styles is critical. A person's behavioral style is how she perceives and handles information and how she reacts to other people and different situations. It is essentially the basic difference in how people act and respond to their environment and the larger world around them.

The successful leader understands that she must cultivate and nurture effective relationships to be effective. Leaders have to put their efforts into motivating and inspiring people rather than focusing on control and command. The focus is on recognizing the unique attributes that each person brings to the task and eliminating (as much as possible) prejudices, assumptions, preconceived notions, or judgments about people. Appreciating the differences and unique contributions of those around them is a key strength of successful leaders. You can operate more effectively when you recognize the particular behavioral styles of those around you. When you understand the different behavioral styles, you acquire the mindset necessary to appreciate each individual.

A key element of how we create our individual styles is *selective perception*. Your experiences, beliefs, interests, and values are all part of what makes up your selective perception filter. This filter draws your attention to certain aspects of the world that conform to your experience, while excluding those aspects that don't fit. For example, when you shop for a new car you select the particular model you want because of its style, color, and other individual characteristics. At the time of your purchase, you hadn't seen another car like it anywhere. Suddenly, after you buy yours, you see the same car everywhere. You didn't copy anyone else, and they certainly didn't imitate you. What happened?

The other cars have been there all along, but because you didn't have a particular interest in them, your selective perception filter excluded them from your attention. Once you had personalized the make, model, and color, the filter adjusted to include the previously invisible automobiles. Your selective perception filter works the same way with the rest of your world. There is always the tendency to either lock information out or lock it in, because of what we expect.

What do you see in the following image?

At first, you may see only a vase, or you may see only two faces. If you tend to see the vase (the white part of the image) you may have trouble seeing the faces (the black part) and vice versa. You do the same thing in life. Human beings tend to see only what their selective perceptions have been conditioned to see.

Once you understand that each of us sees the world differently because of our selective perception filter, you can focus on those activities that work best with each individual. Recognizing that you have your own filter, you can work to overcome any blind spots that you may have. It is much more difficult to understand and accept the differences in individuals if you don't realize that you've seen them through your own selective perception filter.

When we speak of behavioral "styles," the possible combinations are endless, as each of us is a complex individual. However, you will be more comfortable and more effective using one style, and the techniques, strengths, and weaknesses of that style will dominate your behavior.

For working purposes, then, it is a good idea to come up with some categories of behavioral styles, or dimensions, so that you can consciously work with your strengths. By understanding your behavioral styles, you and your partners can then assign the appropriate roles based on the categories. The behavioral style matrix is a useful tool to help you understand the points of view of various personalities. Behavioral styles are broken down into four primary types. All of us display characteristics of each style at different times, but every individual tends to be dominant in one style. The dominant style and the elements of that style are how we identify individuals. The four primary behavioral styles are ***Controlling, Supporting, Promoting,*** and ***Analyzing***.

The *Controlling* style is often the classic type A personality. This person is goal- and result-oriented, she focuses on the bottom line, and she rushes in fearlessly to take on whatever challenge is in front of her. To the Controller, instant decisions and instant execution are the best methods to solve any problem.

To say the Controller is decisive is an understatement. The Controller quickly analyzes the situation, determines a course of action, and takes off. Usually the Controller is a step ahead of everyone else because of the quick decision making. Even if the decision is not the best solution, the Controller gets things done through sheer energy and will.

Because Controllers believe so heavily in action, they are businesslike and task oriented. They like it best when they have a full plate—too much to do and not enough time to do it. A list of chores that would intimidate other people and which they would find impossible to get accomplished is what the Controller craves.

Controllers are self-motivated, competent, and determined. Due to their ability to get things done, Controllers draw heaps of praise from others. On paper, the Controller can't be beat. She makes a list of achievements, and she leads everyone else. However, the Controller doesn't necessarily need the encouragement. Forceful and with a sense of urgency, the Controller can get things done with a minimum of support.

An effective way to communicate with a Controller partner is the most direct way, thus saving time and providing clear communication. Phrase your questions and comments so the Controller does not have to give up power or control. For example, it is not effective to tell a Controller, "I would like to change our company vision and do it this way." A more effective way to get the buy-in from the Controller is to phrase the question so it is less threatening to her sense of control. Try this: "Do you think we could change our company vision and do it this way?"

One aspect of the Controller that can be very useful in a partnership is her willingness to confront others when necessary. Unfortunately, in her eagerness to get the job done, the Controller can forget tact and offend those around her. The very directness that can in some circumstances prove useful can, to some people, make the Controller come across as impatient and demanding.

The Controller sets very high standards for herself and expects the same high standards from others. When others don't perform as the Controller expected, she can easily become frustrated and critical of their performance. Although a doer herself, the Controller may lose patience with someone who works differently than she does. Anyone who is slow on the uptake or slow to get a task done will quickly discover the wrath of the Controller.

Because the Controller is a person of action, she may come across as demanding and impatient. Results matter to the Controller, and her sense of urgency can sometimes lead to poor delegating skills. She may take over a task assigned to someone else simply to get it done. The Controller, as you might imagine from the name, relishes being in charge and resents others having power over her.

The *Promoting* style provides the energy that everyone else can feed off of. The Promoter enjoys exciting activities that involve movement and action. The Promoter thrives on providing motivation and inspiration—both to himself and to others. The Promoter tends to be imaginative and creative in getting desired results. He is a risk taker.

You would call the Promoter a *"people person."* Naturally outgoing and energetic, he gets excited easily and finds it easy to inspire and motivate those around him. Because of this charisma, the Promoter tends to be a natural leader. His persuasiveness makes people want to do things for him.

Promoters thrive on changing circumstances and new challenges. They are quick decision makers, and they will change their course of action quickly when they see that what they are doing isn't working. Because of their ability to motivate others, they can take the discouragement out of setbacks, reframing the situation so that it provides exciting new opportunities for the team.

Unfortunately, because of their quick decision making, Promoters are sometimes guilty of poor planning. Excitement can take a project only so far before their lack of follow-through and concern over details can stop it in its tracks. The Promoter's optimism sometimes prompts them to start more things than they can finish, which can frustrate those around them.

Because of their eternal optimism, Promoters can tend to exaggerate, sometimes hurting their credibility. They will often jump to conclusions too quickly, making their judgment suspect. Those who have to work with the Promoter will find themselves in a position of having to verify what they're told so they can move ahead on a project.

In a partnership scenario, the Promoter is the visionary and can outdo anyone else when it comes to creating new ideas or solving problems. He is best fit to handle the creative aspects of the company, including marketing and public relations. Promoters are natural salespeople and are great at creating programs that attract customers, clients, and sales leads. The Promoter can also be a great inspirational leader of a company if other partners take on the role of keeping the leader focused and on task.

Often the best way to communicate with a Promoter partner is not to bore him with tasky stuff. Tell him what needs to be done and give him the flexibility to accomplish the project his way. Promoters thrive on creativity and enjoy doing things differently.

The *Supporting* style forms strong, lasting relationships. Supporters are sensitive to other people and are concerned about their feelings; they thrive on human interaction. The Supporter believes in building relationships to get things done.

The Supporter is more likely to listen to what others are saying and use their input to create a win-win solution to problems and conflicts. Because of this ability to connect with people, the Supporter is genuinely concerned with the well-being of others. When the Supporter asks you how you are doing, she means it. *Empathy* is the ability to understand and identify with the feelings, thoughts, and attitudes of others. The Supporter is loaded with empathy and caring for other people. She is more apt to know the names of her co-workers' children and to remember birthdays and other personal details which form the basis for good relationships.

A Supporter can be a very effective business partner. Her good nature and even temper makes her exceptional at resolving conflicts. Merely by having the Supporter involved in a project helps ensure that things will go smoothly. She calms things down, and with a minimum of histrionics and drama the job gets done quicker and easier. Because of the influence of the Supporter, controversy among team members rarely occurs, and it is less severe when it does happen.

Other leaders will often praise the Supporter for her loyalty and support. The Supporter wants to be of service, to be the team player who shows up to work every day and ensures that everything runs smoothly. Cooperative and patient, the Supporter doesn't impose herself on others. Instead, she uses understanding and strong team-building skills to move the entire group and its projects ahead.

The Supporter's need for everything to go smoothly and calmly can be a downside. Conflict is inevitable in any environment when people work together, and the Supporter may go to extraordinary lengths to avoid confrontation or reprimanding others. Being unable to face up to conflict can mean that problem situations get worse for lack of attention. The Supporter may give in to more dominant personalities against her better judgment, simply to avoid confrontation. This same tendency may lead the Supporter to accept less than the best from those around her, lest she appear too demanding.

Finally, the Supporter may feel compelled to wait for approval before making decisions. This can lead to tentativeness, which can be detrimental when decisions need to be made on the spot. The Supporter wants to avoid unpleasantness, especially when she may be reprimanded for making the wrong decision.

The *Analyzing* style places importance on structure and order. The Analyst may welcome change, but only after researching all the possibilities and weighing the consequences before making a decision. The Analyst is conscientious—the type of person who always balances his checkbook. While the other types are interacting with people and running around doing things, the Analyst is setting up systems and structures to help ensure that people are doing what they're *supposed* to be doing.

Every organization and company needs an Analyst. He is the one who make sure that bills are paid, supplies are ordered, and schedules are posted. He has the patience to examine the details of a plan and point out any weaknesses. When the Analyst proposes a course of action, it pays to listen—he uses his exceptional planning skills to weigh different factors before reaching a conclusion.

The Analyst will be the one who uses charts and graphs to illustrate a point. Having given the situation proper consideration, the Analyst will be familiar with the smallest aspects of a plan, and will enjoy showing others what he has learned. The Analyst is persistent and steady, willing to spend whatever time is necessary to come to a reasonable conclusion about any suggestion.

To the Analyst, quality is a priority. If there is a way to quantify quality—through stopwatches, checklists, or other objective measurements—the Analyst will find it. The Analyst will ensure that service and goods are consistently good, and he can prove it. The Analyst can make sure that the company's standards are met and then surpassed. The Analyst can be counted on to follow through on a plan to make sure it's executed properly.

The Analyst is cautious in making decisions because he feels that the most efficient way to do something is to get it right the first time. The Analyst is not driven by instinct—he believes that everything should be backed up by the facts at hand.

The Analyst's obsession with detail can sometimes hold him back. He may become so cautious that he actually becomes an obstacle to the company's goals. Analysts can also be guilty of procrastinating so as to avoid mistakes. This may give the impression that the Analyst is indecisive.

The Analyst can also be resistant to change if the consequences cannot be quantified. He must have data before he can make a decision. When someone else wants to try something innovative and new and there is no history to compare the plan against, the Analyst may withhold support. He doesn't trust his feelings and intuition. Resistance to the plan may be silent, as the Analyst is often hesitant to share his opinion. The Analyst may have trouble deciding when to speak up. One reason the Analyst may be reluctant to speak up is that he is sensitive to criticism. When he can quantify his opinion, he reasons, how can anyone disagree with him? When someone *does* disagree, the Analyst may take it personally and quit participating. To avoid conflict or controversy, the Analyst may simply withdraw under stress.

To be sure, none of us are all of one behavioral type, just as all of us exhibit some of each behavioral type at one time or another. However, one type is usually dominant in how the partners interact with others and in how they listen, respond, comprehend, and perform in various situations. When the partners recognize the strengths and possible weaknesses of each other, it can prevent surprises and make the partnership and the business as strong and profitable as possible.

Entrepreneurial Styles

Just as there are different types of behavioral styles, there are different entrepreneurial styles and personalities. The *entrepreneurial personality* describes how an individual approaches starting, running, and owning his own business. It describes the entrepreneur's tolerance for risk, as well as his desire for reward. Not everyone has the tolerance or mindset to be an entrepreneur. However, entrepreneur types display personality traits that go hand-in-hand with their dominant behavior style. Knowing each partner's approach to entrepreneurship can make each partner stronger. It keeps the partnership working together smoothly and profits both the business and the relationship. As with the behavior styles, cooperation and coordination is made possible by recognizing each other's aptitudes and tendencies.

Any time you try to categorize a personality, there is the tendency to want to pigeonhole the person. Nothing is further from our aim here. Our goal is to point out different possible personality types and to illustrate how each type might work with the other. Human beings are much too complex to categorize completely, and each entrepreneur will have some tendencies toward different styles at different times. However, most people will be more dominant in one of the following categories most of the time. The different types of entrepreneurial styles are as follows:

The All-Rounder. The All-Rounder displays many of the behaviors common to the *Controller* and the *Promoter*. The All-Rounder is the universally responsible entrepreneur, the dynamo who has his fingers in every part of the business. The All-Rounder's versatility is amazing, as he seems to know something about everything. He seems to have picked up various skills at different times in his life, making the All-Rounder one of the handiest people to have around.

The All-Rounder is often a one-person show, serving as his own electrician, carpenter, and plumber, as well as handling all his own accounting, sales, design, production, promotion, and almost every other aspect. When funds are tight at the startup of a business, the company often thrives because of the versatility of the All-Rounder.

The one aspect of the All-Rounder that makes him invaluable is his ability to adapt to change. Of course, everything is new when the business first starts, so conditions change daily. This part is all according to plan. When conditions change and make a redirection—either large or small—to the business plan necessary, the All-Rounder can be counted on to embrace the change and run with it.

Businesses often fail or succeed based on their ability to change. If the owners are too hesitant to make the needed changes, then the business will suffer. Entrepreneurs, like the All-Rounder, will thrive because of their ability to adapt to different conditions. When the company is ready to go in a new direction, you can count on the All-Rounder.

The Organizer. Whereas the All-Rounder is dynamic and hands-on, the Organizer is the administrator. The behavior style of the Organizer includes the traits of the Analyst as well as the Promoter. The Organizer is the one who will create a business plan and apply for all the licenses, certifications, etc., that the business needs to run. The Organizer is more likely to think of herself as an "executive" rather than a laborer.

Although the All-Rounder shows more energy, the Organizer makes sure that her energy is put to its best use. Rational, logical, and able to think things through, the Organizer figures out which direction the business needs to go. She may create a "policies and procedures" manual or a process flowchart to help the business.

When things don't go as expected, the Organizer will analyze the situation and determine what adjustments are needed. Usually preparations have been made for such contingencies—through the Organizer's foresight—and the business simply must correct what went wrong.

The Organizer is a very organized boss, making work easier for her employees. Because she is more of an administrator than a working manager, the Organizer tends to be good at delegating. Employees will learn more and take on more responsibilities as a result of working with the Organizer.

The Routiner. Contrary to the popular image, some entrepreneurs are very cautious. They may recognize that owning their own business is the best way to create more wealth, yet they still want a secure income. When you have an entrepreneur who has small business goals and takes every step carefully, you have the Routiner.

The Routiner is an entrepreneur who displays Supporter and Analyst behaviors. The Routiner is likely to choose businesses that have a proven track record, or which have a very low startup cost. Caution directs all of the Routiner's decisions because he knows that a misstep can be expensive. While the Organizer may take a calculated risk—provided the odds are in his favor—the Routiner eschews risk. "Better safe than sorry" is the Routiner's motto.

With this mindset, the Routiner entrepreneur is not looking to get rich. In fact, he will often set small business goals—an extra *x* amount of extra income a month, for example. If the Routiner's business is a great success, he will expand slowly, if at all, because caution demands that any decisions be prudent ones. Most of all, the Routiner wants a secure income. Anything that endangers the income must be avoided. When the other partners are promoting expansion in the business (which will increase their income), the Routiner will veto the idea because of the unknown consequences. He does not want to commit unnecessarily to anything that might cost him money.

The Pioneer. The Pioneer is the visionary, the one who usually comes up with the initial idea for a business. The Pioneer entrepreneur is actually a Promoter at work. He often displays strong Controller behaviors at times. Almost the complete opposite of the Routiner in temperament, the Pioneer is a risk taker. The bigger the reward, the greater the risk the Pioneer is willing to take. The Pioneer may not be drawn to entrepreneurship strictly because of the money, however; he may want the satisfaction of having his vision realized.

The Pioneer is an innovator—a dynamic, creative entrepreneur. Often it is the satisfaction of creating something that drives the Pioneer. The Pioneer likes doing what has not been done before, and being able to start a successful business is all the validation that the Pioneer seeks.

Each of these types of entrepreneurs can be successful, and each type has strengths that can complement the style of the other partner. Working together, partners can achieve a better understanding of what it takes to make their partnership work.

A Partnership That Failed, a Friendship that Endured (Dan)

As owner of a Martinizing Dry Cleaning franchise, I spent many hours pressing pants and shirts and assembling and bagging clothes. The dry cleaning business is not a business for the weak; the work is hard and time-consuming.

I have personally found the dry cleaning business to be both rewarding and challenging. The challenge for me is the time commitment. I operate multiple businesses, so time is a valuable commodity. Under these considerations, I opted to replace my time with a partner.

After interviewing several possible candidates, I selected a husband–wife team to operate the dry cleaners and a partnership agreement was drafted. This couple had all the right stuff. They were energetic, eager, and entrepreneurial. The partnership arrangement included their commitment to put in a full-time, best-effort managing and operating of the business. They were compensated with a salary and over time would earn equity in the business.

After a few months of operating the business under the agreed partnership, it became obvious that my new partners were having problems in their roles. As true Promoters, they realized that the day-to-day routine was not challenging enough for them. They enjoyed having their hands in a lot of different projects. Spending their full-time best efforts in a dry cleaning business was just too restrictive for their lifestyle.

The partnership had to end. I had a lot of money at stake. My partners were not fulfilling their obligations, so I could have threatened or sued them for my financial losses and hardship. The reality was that this partnership was doomed to fail. A partnership cannot be forced to work; it has to want to work. Instead of dissolving the partnership with lawsuits, legal fees, anger, and frustration, we agreed to dissolve the partnership as friends. Not only did we save thousands of dollars in legal costs, we also retained our friendship and left the door open for a future business deal. Life is too short to create enemies from business mistakes.

"Never hold discussions with the monkey when the organ grinder is in the room."

~ Winston Churchill

CHAPTER FIVE

Can You Hear Me Now?: Effective Communication Strategies

We've all heard about how important "communication" is. Communication is important in the workplace, at home, and in public. Lack of communication is one of the major causes of marital strife. There sometimes seems to be more communication about communication than about anything else. With all the discussion about communication, do we even know what everyone's talking about? Is it possible that, even with everybody talking about communication, we still don't get it? The answer, of course, is a resounding *yes.* Most people don't understand what they need to know about communication.

First of all, what's the definition of communication? When we talk to people at work or at home, aren't we "communicating?" Unfortunately, the answer is *probably not.* If you have misunderstandings, misinterpretations, or a time when one of you simply doesn't "get" what the other is saying, then you're not really communicating.

True communication is *when the meaning of what you want to convey to another person is completely and accurately transmitted and received.* Although it sounds simple, the definition hides a slew of possible obstacles to communication. Otherwise we would all be master communicators, and there would never be any misunderstandings.

Simply the word "meaning," for example, holds massive amounts of subtext. You have the words you speak, for example, plus what the words mean to the person with whom you're communicating. Even if you just stop there, you run into problems. A single word can mean different things to different people, based on their experiences, perceptions, and points of view. Ask several people how they define the words "truth" or "good," and you will get an idea of the complexities involved. Multiply your sampling by every word in your vocabulary, and you have an idea of how big a task it is to communicate effectively.

It's clear, then, that communication is more than simply talking and listening. Although effectively using those two skills will improve your communication drastically, they are just a small part of the arsenal you can use to bolster your communication. Unfortunately, most people have not even mastered those two skills. Because we learn those skills at an early age, we think good speaking and good listening come naturally; but nothing could be further from the truth.

We use communication to transmit ideas. However, even two people who are extremely close and who have a great affinity for one another can have communication breakdown sometimes. The idea—the meaning; the entire package of emotions, images, consequences, and causes—simply doesn't come through clearly.

One of the great stories of the Bible is the story of the Tower of Babel. In the world after the Flood, everyone spoke one language. The citizens of Babylon began to build a tower so immense it would reach into the heavens. God was displeased with this development—a brazen display of man's hubris—so he confused their languages and scattered them across the earth. Notice it wasn't a dramatic thunderbolt that destroyed everything, or some other cataclysmic display of power. The people simply became unable to understand one another.

There are many organizations and companies that suffer from similar situations: the office is full of people, yet no one really understands what the others are doing.

Fortunately, perfect communication is not necessary in order to make progress and to move forward. All the wonders of modern civilization were accomplished by imperfect human beings imperfectly communicating. Everything from the great pyramids of Egypt to the Eiffel Tower to microcircuitry was created using imperfect communication. Not only has communication helped build civilization, it has made civilization possible.

Communication eventually boils down to one person conveying information to another person. It defines relationships. When a couple is having problems, what's one of the first signs? A breakdown in communication. When someone close to us is unnaturally quiet, we notice and ask them what's wrong. In arguments you may scream or say things you don't mean, both examples of poor communication.

On the other hand, when your relationship with another person is strong and secure, you can talk about subjects that are sensitive. You can discuss problems quietly and rationally and work together to find an answer. Nuances of meaning and emotion are understood easily because of the bond between you. Simply making eye contact conveys a lot of information.

One of the standard plots of sitcoms involves a character who misunderstands something another character has said and who becomes twisted in knots trying to assimilate the new, and incorrect, information. Television writers understand how common poor communication works and how mixed-up situations can become because of it. Clearly, then, one of the major goals of good communication is to prevent misunderstandings. While we may never get caught up in some of the silly situations presented on television, we do unnecessarily complicate our lives because of garbled messages. People close to us may get their feelings hurt because of a misunderstanding. Friendships may break up because one of the friends misunderstands something the other has said.

Communicating effectively can prevent and eliminate problems. If we correctly understand one another, we react according to the information we are given. If there is poor communication, then we are reacting according to incorrect information—the information we *thought* we received. And because of the poor communication, the original communicator never realizes something is wrong until it's too late.

With this information, then, it becomes apparent that if we communicate effectively, eliminating misunderstandings and other problems, then we are working more effectively and efficiently. We can move in a straight line directly from problem to solution. Even better, we can move directly to those activities that provide the best return on invested time and energy—the time and energy that would be wasted with poor communication.

If we recognize that effective communication is the ability to convey information clearly and unambiguously *for all parties involved*, then certain points become evident. First of all, listening is as important as speaking, if not more so. As has been pointed out so often, we have two ears and one mouth, and we should use those tools in the same proportion.

We have to pay attention when another person is speaking (or communicating in any other way) because without our attention there is a greater chance that a miscommunication will occur. While listening attentively won't guarantee that there will be no misunderstanding, it greatly improves the odds of a successful communication between the sender and the receiver.

A great way to ensure effective communication is to check for understanding during a conversation by seeking feedback. During any conversation, there should be a series of clues sent back to the speaker from the listener, indicating that he understands. If the speaker feels that there may be a gap in understanding, then he needs to seek feedback to confirm what has been said. This is much more than the habitual "you know what I mean?" or "y'know?" that many people drop mindlessly at the end of every sentence. Seeking feedback means *actively* looking for signs that the listener understands. It means being observant and alert for all of the normal signs of comprehension that the other person exhibits. It means looking for the emotional impact that the conversation is having on the other person.

The most difficult conversations that we have, and the ones that are most often mishandled, are when the subject matter is controversial or critical and when emotions are high. It is ironic that when the subject matter is most important our communicating abilities deteriorate. Our feelings take over, and we focus on our own emotional response rather than on communicating.

In their book *Crucial Conversations: Tools for Talking When Stakes are High*, Patterson et al. discusses the concept of *safety* in a conversation. The authors point out that the free flow of ideas and information in a dialogue can happen only when both parties feel safe. The higher the safety level, the greater the flow of ideas. Many times we engage in conversations while feeling concerned that we will be attacked or humiliated. We focus so much on our own emotions that we can't concentrate on the communication. The lower the safety level (with a higher level of fear), the smaller the flow of ideas.

The authors recommend that you be aware of the "safety level" in a conversation. When you sense that the other person is beginning to feel unsafe—based on the feedback that you look for—or when you begin to feel unsafe yourself, take a moment to turn the atmosphere back to one of safety before continuing. This can be as simple as reassuring the other person of his value to you.

With that in mind, it's important to prepare the environment for the conversation. If there is a high level of tension in the air, the conversation will be more difficult; the conditions are automatically against effective communication. You can prepare the environment by reassuring the other person beforehand and approaching the conversation with heightened awareness of the other person's emotional state, as well as your own.

Although much of the discussion so far has been on oral conversation, there are clearly many additional avenues of communication. In fact, communication is the one area that has exploded with possibilities over the last decade. The rise of the internet—itself a very comprehensive form of communication—and of microelectronics has created a boom in electronic communication.

At its most fundamental level, however, communication involves a face-to-face conversation between two people. In that one simple conversation, there are a number of methods of communication being used. First, you have the words being spoken. Each word has a particular dictionary definition or *denotation*. But words also have *connotation*, the second meaning or subtext that accompanies the denotation. The connotation of language refers to the emotional impact that the word causes in the listener. Connotation also refers to the experience with the word that both the speaker and listener have had. For example, a family might know of a particular food that the children don't like, which becomes a code word for food they don't enjoy when speaking to one another.

Along with the words, part of a conversation is the voice that each speaker uses. The tone, volume, speed of speech, and rate of breathing are all indications that listeners pay attention to in order to determine the speaker's meaning. You need to be aware of your own voice and how it affects other people when you speak. The various elements that make up the tone and inflection of your voice are some of the factors in a conversation you can control.

Another factor in a conversation is your body language. Entire books have been written on interpreting body language, but most people lack the expertise to understand subtle physical cues. Many people use lots of gestures and body movements to convey meaning when they speak (something picked up naturally or culturally) and can throw out false cues to people not adept at reading body language.

In the realm of written communications, of course, factors such as body language are not important. The choice of words was once a major part of written communication, but in this era of email, IMs, and text messages, word usage has become secondary to electronic shorthand. Still, when sending a written communication, think of the context in which the receiver will see the message and what the impact of particular words may have.

While much of this advice applies to both business and personal communication, there are a few thoughts about business communication to keep in mind. First are the legal aspects. A business is a legal entity, and you have to assume that any communications you have with partners or employees may wind up being used in a legal proceeding. An off-the-cuff remark to a subordinate could wind up as a discrimination complaint. A statement made to a partner could be construed as a contract. Also, when communicating in business it's always a good idea to make all communications in a professional manner. Besides the aforementioned legal implications, the way you communicate tells other people a lot about your level of professionalism. A sloppily-written note full of misspelled words and grammatical errors sends a definite message about you—one that you may not intend.

In that same vein, business communications should deal with business subject matter. Personal matters are better left to personal communications. It's never a good idea to mix the two because someone may misunderstand whether your intentions have to do with business or personal matters. Confusion in a business communication is one result that you absolutely *don't* want.

One similarity in both personal and business communication, however, is that when there is a strain, communication is the first thing to suffer. In both instances keep an eye on the level of communication, and that can tell you if there are other problems that need to be addressed. Of course, the only way to discover what those problems are is by *communicating.*

When difficulties seem to be arising, effective communication is the first step to resolving the issue. Regardless of the problem, finding a solution will be easier if both partners agree to some basic principles regarding communication. First, both partners must agree that communication is important. Remaining silent when trying to solve a problem is neither an effective way to communicate nor an effective way to resolve the problem. When both parties in a dialogue agree that communication is important, they can overcome any obstacles that may arise in the course of the conversation.

Partners must also agree to ground rules that keep the dialogue moving forward. In order to have a productive conversation, they must:

1. **Stay on the subject.** No good comes of bringing up immaterial grudges from the past while trying to resolve the current issue.
2. **Listen for understanding.** You have to actually be listening to what the other person is saying so you can be sure that you are staying on the subject.
3. **Adapt your behavior.** Be flexible and adapt your behavior to ensure that you're both communicating effectively and supporting each other by staying on the subject.

Finally, remember to put safety into the communication environment. Stressful conversations can be handled productively if each party has resolved to let the other keep his dignity and if everyone involved feels respected as a participant.

As we mentioned earlier, listening effectively is one of the most important aspects of good communication. When you're listening attentively, you indicate that you are receptive and ready to understand what the other person is saying. It shows a preparedness to actually hear the other person's point of view. One of the habits in Stephen Covey's book *The 7 Habits of Highly Effective People* is "Seek first to understand, and then to be understood." As you enter into a dialogue with another person, remember the basics: listen for emotion and subtext to what the other person is saying. Listen for *connotation* as well as *denotation*.

When it is your turn to speak, try to augment the effectiveness of your communication by considering the other person's behavior style. That means you have to *talk for understanding*. When you talk for understanding, you complement the way the other person listens and processes information. You look for feedback in emotion as well as in words and meaning.

What happens when you don't talk for understanding? You increase the risk of misunderstanding and incomprehension. You wind up feeling that what you said "went in one ear and out the other." Such a conversation frustrates both you and the person you're speaking to.

When you make the effort to talk for understanding, you show sympathy as well as respect for the listener. You give equality to both sides of the dialogue and ensure that the matter being discussed is resolved in the manner most satisfactory to all parties. When you take into consideration the way the other person processes information, or learns, it shows that you think enough of him and of the situation that you are giving it serious attention.

It is not surprising to discover that people learn in different ways. *Neurolinguistic Programming*, or *NLP* for short, is a model of how people communicate with themselves and with other people. Developed by Richard Bandler and John Grinder, NLP explains how individuals process information and how that process manifests itself in their communications. Although everyone exhibits some characteristics of each type of learning, there are four primary learning styles: *Auditory, Visual, Kinesthetic,* and *Auditory-Digital.*

Auditory. As you might imagine by the name, auditory learners absorb information best by listening. In school they were the ones who did best on oral exams or who learned more from lectures than from their reading. When they *did* read, they liked to read aloud. They often were the best at speaking in front of the class.

The auditory learner often exhibits behaviors that indicate her learning style. During a conversation, she may repeat what you've said back to you; doing this helps her retain the information. She follows oral instructions better than written instructions. Her preferred method of communication is face-to-face or by telephone, so that she can hear your voice.

There may be conversational clues that you are dealing with an auditory learner. Some phrases she might use includes:

"Can you say that again?"
"Just tell me the facts."
"Did I hear you correctly?"
"It sounds to me like ..."

If you want to communicate better with an auditory learner, use techniques that emphasize sound, noise, or oral communication. You might use rhymes to help the auditory learner remember facts. Repeating key phrases aloud that you want her to remember can help her retain information. You might preface an important point with "I want you to hear what I'm saying," or even a quick "Listen up."

What you want to avoid with the auditory learner is relying too heavily on written or visual techniques. A video without explanatory dialogue or narration can confuse her. If you hand her written instructions, she may ask you to go over it with her aloud. Charts and pictures just bore her; instead, give her a recording of what you want her to know and she will learn it faster and have better retention.

Visual. The visual learner is almost the complete opposite of the auditory learner. Oral instructions may not be retained, whereas being able to read them makes the information clearer to the visual learner. The visual learner is the good reader, the one who can describe the scenes in a novel or in a movie. The visual learner is the person who will read the instructions before putting a model or a piece of equipment together. He learns best by using his eyes.

The visual learner will give you clues as to his learning style. When you are discussing something that is written, he may ask to look at it so he can read it himself—even if you have already explained it. When explaining something to others, he will often sketch a diagram, picture, or graph to illustrate his point. He will watch you as you speak to him, looking for extra information in your face or gestures. Visual learners love using memos, letters, emails, and other written forms of communication.

There are also conversational clues that you're dealing with a visual learner. You might hear him say some of the following phrases:

> *"Show me what you mean."*
> *"It looks to me like…."*
> *"I don't believe my eyes."* (They don't really mean this!)
> *"Can I see that again?"*
> *"Just show me the facts."*

If you want to communicate better with a visual learner, *show* him what you mean. During conversation, use lots of gestures and facial expressions to illustrate your point. Preface important points by saying "Look here …" When you can, use written materials to augment other forms of communication. Use images such as photographs, charts, or graphs in your explanations.

When you can, avoid long lectures or talks without some form of visual stimulation. The visual learner will only become bored. Don't try to carry on a conversation in a noisy environment, as noise distracts the visual learner. Don't ask the visual learner to do something new without having provided some sort of written notes or instructions. A well-written manual is the visual learner's best friend.

Kinesthetic. The kinesthetic learner processes information physically, according to how she *feels* about it. Neither auditory nor visual methods are the best way to work with the kinesthetic learner. She is a "hands-on" learner who processes information by doing. In school, the kinesthetic learner was probably good at sports, shop, and other activities that involved using her hands.

Some clues you might get that you are dealing with a kinesthetic learner include how she wants to "jump in" when learning something new. She might be fidgety and unable to sit still, always eager to get busy doing something active. The kinesthetic learner will often raise her hand when someone needs a volunteer for a demonstration. She is a toucher and feeler, using tactile methods to learn.

The kinesthetic learner is often also more in tune with her emotions and the physical manifestation of her feelings. She may associate information with the passion and emotion with which you communicate it. She may make decisions based on intuition rather than waiting for all the facts.

There are conversational cues that you are dealing with a kinesthetic learner. You might hear phrases like these:

> *"Would you share the facts with me?"*
> *"I have a bad feeling about this."*
> *"Let's stay in touch."*
> *"How do you feel about this?"*

If you want to communicate more effectively with a kinesthetic learner, give her a chance to put her hands to work; let her learn the skill by doing, by physically reproducing results, or by using physical models to demonstrate concrete ideas. Keep lessons short to accommodate the kinesthetic learner's tendency to lose focus and start fidgeting. Give the kinesthetic learner room to move when you speak to her. During a conversation, try to express ideas by associating them with emotions.

What you want to avoid is long sessions of watching and/or listening for the kinesthetic learner, without giving her a chance to participate. Don't be cold or unemotional when speaking with her, and don't squelch her need to express her emotions. Don't try to communicate for very long in a cramped, closed environment; the kinesthetic learner needs room to move and express her thoughts.

Auditory-Digital. The auditory-digital learner eschews different sensory-based methods of learning and then compares what he hears to known facts. The auditory-digital learner looks for the underlying meaning and uses logical thought processes to assimilate the new knowledge. Since he needs to mull things over in his mind, don't look for him to be spontaneous.

The auditory-digital learner will give you conversational cues indicating his system for processing information. He may use phrases like these:

> *"That makes sense to me."*
> *"That's a logical idea."*
> *"The data supports that idea."*

When dealing with the auditory-digital learner, use data to back up your own points. Numbers, statistics, and proven facts are the best tools to present to the auditory-digital learner. Try to remove emotion from your points, and remember that your opinions have to be logical. The process you used to get to your opinion will be important to the auditory-digital learner.

As with the previously mentioned categories, types, and styles, all of us use all of these systems at one time or another; however, we are more comfortable using one more often than the others. All of the systems are excellent tools for communicating with others and should be available for you to use when you need them.

It's important that you use your new knowledge to determine your own communication style and the style of your partner. When you speak to your partner, you will know that you are communicating effectively—talking for understanding and not simply "talking to a brick wall."

Communication—A Tool for Understanding (Manon)

I believe that getting people to talk about what they are thinking is a key to better understanding, which leads to better communication. When a partner or employee has done something that you know is wrong, it is easy to point fingers, reprimand, scold, or accuse. This type of behavior may give the accuser an immediate sense of power. However, it puts the employee or partner in a defensive state of mind that can lead to resentment and a hostile work environment.

During our years as a McDonald's restaurant owner, we had the pleasure of working with a woman named Sylvia who worked for the corporation and served as our business consultant. Her job was to enforce the company's standard operating procedures. In layman's terms, she was an inspector—a "cop" for the corporation. She could easily have pointed fingers and degraded us to show her power. Instead, she had a wonderful technique that she used to gain understanding first. When she observed a procedure or technique that was not appropriate, she would ask the question, "Help me understand why you did it that way?"

What a great way to take the pressure off of the situation and stay open to understanding. Once she was given an explanation, it was easier for her to coach, train, and make corrections.

It is easy to do a little detective work by asking, "Help me understand why—?" You will avoid making assumptions and you will be respected for caring enough to ask why a certain action was taken. This communication tool is a real win-win. We will always be grateful to Sylvia for teaching us this valuable lesson.

"I am free of all prejudices. I hate everyone equally."

~ W. C. Fields

CHAPTER SIX

The Irresistible Force Meets the Immovable Object: Confrontation and Conflict Resolution

"Into each life some rain must fall," wrote Henry Wadsworth Longfellow. If he had been in business with a partner, he would have written the corollary, "In each partnership there will be conflict." In any relationship between two people, no matter how close or how affectionate, there will come times when the partners disagree on something. It may be over something small, something large, or something small that becomes something large, but it will happen. How the partners handle the conflict is a determining factor in how successful the partnership will be.

According to the Small Business Administration (SBA), 50 percent of all business partnerships fail; often a result of an unresolved conflict between partners. Although there are many ways to get into a conflict with a partner, there are only a few ways to get out. To reach a mature resolution, both partners must agree to resolve the conflict, either with or without the help of a third party. If one of the partners decides for some reason that he doesn't want to resolve the conflict, then there is no longer a partnership—it has become an antagonistic relationship. There is a spectrum of conflict resolution, depending on the depth of the conflict and the input the partners receive from third parties.

- **Negotiation**. This is the preferred method of conflict resolution. The partners discuss their respective positions, and they come to a solution that is acceptable to both.
- **Facilitation**. Sometimes the partners need a third party to help them in their discussion. With a facilitator's help they engage in negotiation and find a solution. This is negotiation made easier.
- **Mediation**. Both partners present their cases to a third party—a *mediator*—who listens and makes recommendations for a solution, which may or may not be accepted by the partners.
- **Counseling**. The partners seek the help of a professional, who offers advice based on the personalities of the partners, with less regard to the actual merits of their arguments.
- **Expert advice**. The partners seek the help of an expert on the factors of the conflict. The expert focuses on the facts of the case, with little or no input on the personalities of the partners.
- **Arbitration**. This is similar to mediation except that the arbitrator's decision, although made outside the legal system, can be legally binding.
- **Litigation**. This is the last resort. It involves the legal system, courts, and lawyers; it is nasty and expensive.

In most cases, negotiation is all that's needed to resolve a conflict between partners. When each of them has an investment in the partnership, they realize that it is more profitable and productive to work out whatever conflicts they have. Few disputes are worth the loss of relationships and money that a protracted lawsuit or disagreement would cost.

When resolving disputes, it's helpful to have guidelines. Guidelines help ensure that the conflict takes up the least amount of resources as you work toward resolution. Following are some guidelines that partners should agree to when trying to resolve a dispute.

First, agree on and clarify all the issues in dispute. Many times partners will find themselves in a struggle over different things. Poor communication leads to this phenomenon, and simply discussing the issues and clarifying what each partner is saying can resolve the conflict.

Next, emphasize that each person has ample opportunity to share his opinions. This means that no one leaves the session feeling as though he has not had input into the resolution. Often 99 percent of the issue is really not in conflict, and the small part that's left can be easily resolved. However, the partners can discover this only if everyone has their say. This also means that each participant must practice active listening skills so that the exchange of knowledge is complete.

Collect facts and data. Conflicts are often the result of incomplete knowledge on the part of one of the people involved. It should be the duty of each partner to bring to the table whatever pertinent facts or data he has. Once the facts have been displayed, the partners may find that they are in agreement on the matter.

After the data has been collected, list the pros and cons of each person's position. Seeing each of the possible points in writing can enlighten someone as to something they hadn't considered. When the pros and cons are listed side by side, it often becomes clear that one of the options far outweighs the other.

You may also want to identify alternatives. This is where creativity and flexibility are key. Try to find solutions that have maximum advantages and minimum drawbacks. The resolution of the conflict may be an option that is different from what anyone had brought to the meeting.

After going through this process, there needs to be an agreement or consensus on what represents the best solution. One of the most important requirements for satisfactory conflict resolution is the willingness to compromise. It's not a mature, or realistic, expectation to get your way 100 percent of the time. It's not realistic to expect to get 100 percent of your way *most* of the time. Such an immature viewpoint leaves no room for partnership. Being true "partners" means that all partners should give input into any given situation. Two people never make one decision. It is your responsibility to make the decisions that fall within your job role. It is the job of your partners to respect and support your decisions. This is called true partnership. When you make decisions unilaterally—outside the scope of your job role, of course—then you don't have a true partnership. If you are unwilling to compromise, it means that the partnership has become secondary to you getting your way.

In a partnership, "my way or the highway" won't work. Ultimatums are one of the surest ways to destroy a relationship. If the partnership is worth saving, then you have to find alternatives to ultimatums. As they say, "it takes two to tango."

When both partners enter into a situation willing to bend, to compromise, it makes for a stronger partnership. Each of the partners realizes that the other puts the partnership above personal feelings or pride. The relationship improves because of this flexibility. Additionally, when both partners exhibit their willingness to compromise, conflicts are actually avoided, because each partner is willing to listen to the other's ideas. When both are willing to compromise, and a solution is found, each of the partners has ownership of the decision. That ownership gives each partner responsibility for the consequences so that later on neither can play the "blame game" by pointing a finger at the other.

Sometimes, one partner will have a more powerful personality than the other. One partner may be more articulate, more intelligent, or more organized. The danger when this situation occurs is that the stronger partner may persuade the other partner into submission. Although presenting facts and data is important, when persuasion is misused it becomes a unilateral attack against one partner. This type of persuasion is not an effective method in resolving conflict. The partner who has been "persuaded" may simply be eager to escape the argument. At that point the situation is actually worse than before because the stronger partner believes that the conflict has been resolved. The persuaded partner merely feels bullied. Although the confrontation itself has been resolved short-term, the spirit of partnership has been damaged.

When one partner is persuaded and forced to submit or to accept the other partner's solution, it breeds resentment and provokes retaliation. The focus has shifted from the original problem to the treatment that the partner received. When outgunned in one area, the partner may feel compelled to strike back in another area where he perceives the stronger partner can be hurt. At this point, the conflict has become a battle.

If you feel that persuasion is necessary, enter into it gently and with a loving, caring spirit. Value the partner more than the decision. If you provide facts, back them up with the pros and cons, and show a willingness to compromise, the other partner can still feel respected. When a solution or resolution is found, both partners should feel ownership for the decision.

It's clear that flexibility is a key component of a successful partnership. You must be willing to change your ways if the situation calls for it. No one has a right to be inflexible simply because "we've always done it that way." Although there may be strong similarities with previous experiences, and you want to bring what knowledge and experience you have to bear on a situation, you need to realize that in reality each situation is brand new, with its own set of circumstances.

A successful partnership thrives when the partners:

- Are willing to compromise and consider other point of views
- Demonstrate flexibility and are open to change
- Share common goals
- Respect and support each others decisions

Most conflicts can be resolved when each of the partners know that the other is willing to be flexible. That knowledge provides the "safety" in the situation mentioned in the book *Crucial Conversations.* Knowing that they don't have to surrender their point lets partners relax and focus on resolving the problems rather than defending themselves.

When it comes to a partnership, stubbornness needs to be checked at the door. Being hardheaded and unwilling to bend may be the number one cause of partnership failure. There is simply no room for it in a partnership.

When it comes to actually handling a conflict, language is the most important—and potentially devastating—tool that you have at your disposal. Especially when you are passionate about a subject, it's vital that you choose your words wisely to avoid unintended consequences. Remember that it's the situation you want to attack, not the other person. Choose your words so that you mention the issue without attacking the other person or his viewpoint. Emphasize this point as you put forth your arguments—that the issue is what you want to correct, not your partner.

It's often a good idea to frame your argument in the form of questions. The words "What if …" are magical in their ability to open up new ideas and viewpoints. The question "Help me understand ..." can have powerful results. For example, do not ask, "Why did you order that merchandise?" Rather, ask your partner, "Help me understand why you chose to order that merchandise." Asking for understanding simplifies the process of focusing on the issue at hand rather than on your partner. Also, asking for understanding gives the partner an opportunity to think and clarify his position. And, he may even realize that his decision was not the wisest. (Note: when we say "questions," we mean real questions where you wait for an answer, not an accusation that simply has a question mark at the end.)

Especially when emotions are running high, it is easy to fall into using destructive language and comments. *Destructive* means words and phrases that work against resolution of the situation and which instead focus on the faults you perceive in your partner. Besides its ineffectiveness, the problem with destructive language is that it goes straight into the long-term memory of whoever you're using it against. Forgiveness may come, but you can be assured that *your* hard words will not be forgotten.

Here are some phrases that can cause long-lasting harm:

> *"You're stupid if you do it this way."*
> *"Sometimes I get so frustrated with you."*
> *"You messed up again."*

While it is acceptable and useful to attack the situation, don't use the circumstances to launch an attack against the other person. Hot emotions can cause you to edge into blurring your attack, subtly phrasing it so that it begins to include your partner. Be aware of your own emotional state, and don't fall into that kind of behavior. It will only hurt the partnership in the long run.

When frustrations, anger, and disappointment bubble over into your statements, take a breath, refocus, and verbalize with gentle language. You want to express yourself in a way that does not attack your partner. Here are some examples:

- "I strongly believe that my way of doing this project is better. Can you help me understand why you think your way is better?"
- "I am feeling frustrated. Can you help me understand why you handled the situation the way you did?"
- "I am disappointed in the results of your efforts on the project. What do you plan to do differently next time so you succeed?"

Remember to keep in mind how much you value your partner. Let your affection and love reflect itself in your language.

The reason that you chose a partner originally—whether in business or in your personal life—is because you believed that person would be able to complement your life. In other words, by having your partner you would be able to accomplish more, achieve more, and enjoy life more. You can harness that additional power of the partnership by being a thoughtful, flexible partner yourself.

Keep in mind that not everyone sees the world the way you do. One of the signs of being an emotionally mature adult is the ability to step outside of yourself and look at a situation through your partner's eyes. There's an old saying, "You can't really understand another person's experience until you've walked a mile in his shoes." If you put forth the sincere effort to understand your partner's point of view, you may discover that he is right after all.

By showing empathy, you can clarify your own understanding. Often this results in a quicker resolution of the conflict, or even a total avoidance of the conflict. It is stunning what effects seeking to understand another person can have on your own point of view. It's as though a heavy curtain has been drawn from a window and the sunlight illuminates areas that were previously hidden in darkness.

Remember to respect your partner's opinions, suggestions, and perspectives. You must entertain the notion that they are right and you are wrong. If you can keep that thought in mind, you may relax your rigid stance and be able to think of different solutions. As Ray Kroc, Founder of McDonald's Corporation, often said, "None of us is as good as all of us." Alternative viewpoints are an asset to any business because they allow you to harness the exponential power of partnership. Synergistic solutions—ideas that result from an informed, honest, and open discussion of the situation—are often better than anything that either of the partners brought to the table originally.

If you accept that there is no such thing as a perfect human being, it's easier to accept that there is no such thing as a perfect partner. We all make mistakes, we all have accidents, and we all make errors in judgment. The point with a partner is that he will make mistakes that are different from the ones *you* make. When you have your own lapses in judgment, don't you hope that your partner will be forgiving and understanding?

That's why it is important to choose partners wisely and to assign to them roles for which they are suited. If you throw someone into a position in which he has no training and no experience, it's unrealistic to expect him to be error-free in his actions. It is better to find the proper fit for his particular set of skills, knowledge, and abilities so that he can contribute immediately and be successful in what he does.

Whoever your partner is, remember that he means well, and that he wants the partnership to succeed as much as you do. Don't attribute ill intentions where there are none. Many times you may start to take their errors personally, as though they were made to purposely hurt you. Take situations where your partner has not performed as well as you wanted for what they are: a simple matter of good intentions that didn't live up to your expectations.

Most of us are doing the best job we know how. Variable circumstances sometimes combine with personal deficiencies, and that's what causes errors, mistakes, and poor judgment. Even people who are proficient make mistakes. Professional tennis players double fault, Tiger Woods misses putts, major league baseball players swing and miss.

What is important about your partner is the same as with the professional athletes. *They are all in the game to win.* The pros understand that there will be another game some other day where they can do better. Your partner will also have other situations in which his expertise and skill may save the day for the partnership. Making mistakes is not a character flaw. The same goes for you. You cannot beat yourself up over mistakes that you may have made, and you can't allow others to do it to you. You are doing the best that you know how, and your intentions are honorable. Forgive the trespasses of others the way that you forgive yourself.

Questioning the integrity of a partner is one destructive action that leaves scars. The relationship of the individuals involved in the partnership should be unassailable. Never threaten a relationship—that's an attack that cannot be taken back or apologized for after the words have been said. Similarly, negativity will destroy a partnership. It brings shame to the partner who introduces it, and it can shame a partner who retaliates with it. The partnership was started with positive energy, with the hope that good things would result from its efforts. If a situation has deteriorated to the point where the partners are engaging in negative actions, then the partnership has suffered damage that needs to be repaired. The primary problem is not the purported issue that separates the partners, but rather their attitude toward the partnership itself.

An effective partnership is a three-legged stool, supported by open communication, honesty, and trust. Honesty should be a given, both in business dealings and in the personal relationship between partners. Lies and deception are destructive to human interactions at any time, and are simply amplified when they occur in a business partnership. Trust is a quality that should be given unreservedly at first and then earned by the one being trusted. You earn trust by being *trustworthy*—by keeping promises to others and to yourself, by telling the truth, and by responsibly handling the role that you have been assigned. Making an honest mistake does not make you untrustworthy.

Open communication is the tool that lubricates the interactions between people. Mature partners let others know when a problem is beginning to bother them, and they pay attention when someone else makes the same claim. Communicating effectively is important also, of course, but legitimate, honorably motivated communication is the prerequisite for keeping a partnership successful. Effectiveness comes with practice and learned technique; proper motivation comes from the heart.

Ultimately, business partnerships are personal partnerships as well, and it's important to keep business and personal life as separate as possible. We go into business to improve our lives, not the other way around. You can't allow the business to become your life. When you keep your business and personal lives in balance, you lower stress and become a kinder, more tolerable partner. The one improves the other. Keeping both aspects balanced ensures that you are able to maximize your effectiveness and are better able to handle issues that arise.

Going into business for yourself carries a lot of rewards: higher self esteem, independence, self sufficiency, possibly wealth, and financial security—but all of these are secondary to the rewards of leading a successful personal life. The rewards that being an entrepreneur earns you are meant to augment your personal life and the lives of your family and those you care for.

Monitoring your own attitudes about family and business is vital. Occasional imbalances are necessary, of course, because you want to focus on one thing at a time. When you find that your business partnership has become more important to you than your personal partnerships, however, then that's a sign that you have lost perspective and your priorities are out of whack.

Conflicts are not necessarily a sign that things are going badly in your relationships. They can be indicators that everyone involved feels respected and valued and considers themselves contributors to the partnership. They feel safe in expressing their honest opinions about a given situation. How we handle conflicts, however, illustrate the relative health of the relationships and the importance that we place on the people around us. A partner who handles conflicts maturely and effectively shows that he has the balance in his life that a good partnership requires. The need to handle conflicts is the reason why minors are not allowed to enter into legal contracts. Children are not emotionally mature enough to consider the consequences and responsibilities that a commitment to a partnership requires.

Conflicts are inevitable, yes, but disasters and tragedy resulting from those conflicts are not. The process of working through conflict can help the partners develop their own interpersonal skills and can bring out better solutions than either partner brought to the table originally. The way we view conflict, then, illustrates how we view life in general. If you view conflict as a win-or-lose competition between partners, someone will inevitably suffer because of it. If you think of conflict as a way for you to grow, for you to temper the steel of your character, then conflict resolution can benefit your personal life tremendously.

"There's no easy way out. If there were, I would have bought it. And believe me, it would be one of my favorite things!"

~ Oprah Winfrey

CHAPTER SEVEN

Begin with the End in Mind: Values, Missions, and Goals

We often hear about a company's "goals." In the media, financial analysts talk about a company's goals and spokespeople appear on television to tout goals. With all this talk about goals, it should seem clear what goals actually are, but do you know for sure? And if you already have goals, how can you make sure they are the right ones?

In this chapter we will discuss three different areas: values, mission statements, and goals. A partnership should spend time on all three since all of them are vital to a healthy partnership and a healthy business. However, they are all different from one another, so we will discuss them each in order.

Values

Every company has values, whether they are explicitly stated or not. Values are the standards of behavior that the business—employees, partners, and representatives—follows when it conducts business. For most companies, the values are expressed loosely, if at all. Many times everyone does whatever they want, without taking conscious thought of the company's values.

It would be much more productive and constructive if, before the business was ever opened, values could be settled on. Instead of haphazard actions, a business should have an expression of the qualities it wants to exhibit in all its behavior. This document (and we've already discussed the importance of writing things down) is called a *value statement.*

Before discussing the value statement, however, let's define what values are. They are the standards you want to adhere to in all of your actions. They are like instructions for behavior when you don't have precise instructions. They are the moral laws that everyone in the business should follow when they start to do something. The standards for your company's values should be high. You want to appeal to the best nature of your people and urge them to strive for the highest standard of behavior. Perfection in reaching these values is never possible, but the pursuit of high values means that both partners and employees will engage in high-level activities. Anyone involved in such a pursuit will automatically show more energy and do a better job.

What kind of values should a business or a partnership have? That depends on the individuals. One of the top values might be honesty. Honesty is a fundamental quality that any businessperson can agree on. Respect for others is another good value for a business. Everyone—partners, employees, customers, vendors, or anyone who is a stakeholder—wants to be respected. Another good value for a business might be profitability. Profitability sustains the business, making it possible to express the other values on your list. As has often been said, "No margin, no mission." When this value is expressed at every level, even the newest employee will find it easier to make decisions when she realizes that it costs the business money. Other possible values are quality and customer satisfaction. You may define and refine these terms however you want so that they adhere to your individual circumstances, but few companies stay in business for very long if they ignore these two values. Customers universally want to see these values expressed in the way you run your business.

Once you've decided on your values, it's time to create a *value statement*. A value statement is a written expression of corporate morality, the values that the company holds most dear. The value statement is the foundation upon which all decisions and actions of the business are based.

The value statement should include a definition of the values, in the highest terms possible. A value statement is designed to set standards, and setting high standards creates a climate in which all participants can do their best work and achieve their highest goals. The value statement creates a map of expected behavior, removing doubts that anyone might have about what is expected of them. A value statement should not include specific goals or objectives. It should include words and descriptions that clarify the moral standards and ultimate vision of the business or partnership. For example, the value statement may include phrases such as "recognized as the industry leader," "uncompromised ethical standards," and "honesty and integrity."

What happens if you don't have a value statement? There will inevitably be a loss of energy and direction, because employees and partners alike will be confused as to what is expected of them. Without a moral guide, there is no restriction on behavior, which can only be destructive to the business. Resources will be squandered because of lack of focus. On the other hand, having a value statement expressing the highest values of the company can energize and motivate employees. They can take pride in the fact that they are working for an organization that strives for the highest level of human behavior. It also removes confusion: whenever explicit instructions have not been given, everyone can refer to the values that they are expected to adhere to.

Mission Statement

Once a value statement has been created, the next step is to create a *mission statement.* A mission statement is the expression of those values in action. The mission statement is an unchangeable belief system that the members of the organization—again, partners, employees, and representatives—can count on and refer to when they have a question about a course of action.

The creation of a mission statement is not to be taken lightly. It should express the way that the company will embrace its values and how they will be demonstrated in the business. Since it is based on fundamental principles and values, it should not need to be changed—unless there has been a dramatic shift in the values that the partners want to exhibit in their business.

The mission statement is a reference guide, a place everyone can look to for direction and instruction. It serves as a guide to acting on values. It answers the question of "how will we embrace our values in the business?" Ultimately, a business is an embodiment of the values it represents and holds dear, and the mission statement is the documentation of that commitment.

The mission statement serves as the hub of a wheel of behavior. Every person in every department should have access to the mission statement and understand that it is the guide for all decisions that they make. Many organizations print their mission statements and hang them on the wall, in nice frames. They want to display their standards of behavior for everyone to see—including vendors, customers, and anyone else who interacts with the business.

What kind of mission statement should a business and a partnership have? That will depend on the individuals involved. Some people make their mission statements detailed and thorough; others word theirs briefly and simply. Regardless of its wording, the mission statement must follow the values that have been established in the value statement.

A mission statement is in alignment with the value statement. However, it includes a more specific agenda for the company, employees, and partners to strive for. For example, the following phrases could be used in a mission statement: "100 percent customer satisfaction," "We're the friendliest business in town," and "If we make a mistake you get the item free."

The company mission statement should also be in harmony with the individual mission statements of everyone involved in its creation. If individuals create mission statements, then the community mission statement should adhere to those, just as it does to the company's values. The mission statement is part of a layered approach to creating a company environment that satisfies everyone involved. It is built on top of the more fundamental beliefs and values of the people involved.

The mission statement will create expectations in the partners, employees, and customers. Rather than lower those expectations by creating a lower-level mission statement, the creators should demonstrate their commitment to the highest possible standards of behavior for everyone in their organization. The mission statement also reflects the culture you want in your business. Without a guide, the culture often deteriorates to the lowest level that you will tolerate. It's better to have the high standards in writing so that all participants know what is expected of them. You can create a culture of trust, respect, and excellence; you are limited only by what you choose to have as your culture.

While the mission statement is unchanging and reflects permanent values, it must not be written in such a way that it can't encompass change. In business, many things can change in a very short period of time. What should not change is the commitment that you and your partners have toward the values that you hold dear. Keep in mind that your business will, if it has any chance of surviving and thriving, go through adjustments and changes. Your mission statement should be able to serve as a guide—without sacrificing any values—whenever your business encounters a new situation.

How do you go about creating a company mission statement? There are a few principles that you need to follow. First, everyone involved should have input into the creation. It is tough getting buy-in from people who are not part of the creation process. As Stephen Covey has written, "People are not committed to the determinations of other people for their lives." Or, as he put it more succinctly elsewhere, "no involvement, no commitment." The process of creating the mission statement is almost as important as the creation itself. A valid mission statement can exist only after much discussion among the participants as to what is really important to them and how they want the company to operate. Deep, moving conversations can happen when people realize that they are working on something important, especially when it involves high concepts like the establishment of basic values in the workplace.

It's probably obvious at this point that the mission statement must have its foundation in the values of the company. Trying to create a mission statement without first establishing values is like trying to build a house on quicksand. No matter how much effort you put into it, it won't have the support that it needs to remain stable. Value-based decisions are the ones that have the greatest chance of success, and the same goes for the creation of your mission statement.

Earlier we mentioned that the mission statement is like the hub of a great wheel. The different departments or areas—marketing, operations, warehousing, etc.—can each have their own mission statement that applies only to their department or area. Each mission statement should be based on the company mission statement, which is itself based on the company's values. It follows that each of the individual mission statements will be based on those same values. They will have the additional benefit of being written to reflect a more refined expression of the values.

The creation of the mission statement should not be another item on the "to-do" list that gets checked off as quickly as possible. This is the one occasion when time should not be a factor. Ensuring the quality of the mission statement is more important than anything else you can be doing with your time. This is the time, before you get involved with the day-to-day running of your business, when you have the opportunity to think, to consider the important activities in your life that give you the most fulfillment.

It's not a crime if you don't have a mission statement. In fact, taking the time to make sure that you have a quality mission statement is more important than trying to rush the process just to make sure you are finished with it. A poorly written mission statement is worse than not having one. Besides that, if you ignore your hastily written mission statement, and everyone else in the organization does too, you will be guilty of hypocrisy. If you went to the trouble of writing a mission statement only to cast it aside when it's inconvenient, then you can't blame anyone for doubting your sincerity and commitment to anything else.

The worst scenario is a mission statement that is ignored. It confuses everyone and creates a problem with situational ethics, where the values and principles of behavior change depending on the situation. In a case like this there is no morality, only unprincipled decisions and behavior. Without an ethical guide, employees are left to fend for themselves when trying to make sense of the company's moral direction.

Goals

After the establishment of your mission statement, it's time to work on your goals. Just as your mission statement was based on your values, your goals need to be based on your values *and* your mission statement. By establishing your goals from the bottom up like this, you can proceed confidently, knowing that you won't run into an ethical conflict anywhere along the way.

What exactly *are* goals, anyway? We can find any number of definitions for goals, but in this context we can say that *a goal is the execution of the expression of your mission statement and your values.* Goals are values in action.

Obviously, setting goals establishes a direction for your actions. When you base your goals on your mission statement and your values, you know that it's the *right* direction. The goals that you set should be designed to further your company's interests and at the same time connect with the values you've established. Like the points on a compass, your values indicate which way you should proceed. In another sense, goals are markers that help keep you on track. In the course of business, there are many distractions and diversions that can take you off course. Without goals to guide you, you can easily find yourself drawn away from what it was you wanted to accomplish. Keeping your goal in mind can help you get back on track and move more directly toward your desired destination.

One way to classify goals is by their timeframe. Long-term goals are strategic, reflecting a general direction for the company. These goals may be in terms of months or even years, depending on your own outlook. Investing in a retirement fund is an example of a long-term goal. When setting such goals you can be more ambitious because you have a long time span in which to accomplish it. Short-term goals may be measured in days, weeks, or months. These goals are more the execution of steps that will eventually lead to the fulfillment of the long-term goals. These goals are very action-oriented and can easily be envisioned. The picture of the completed goal should be clear in your mind when you finish setting the goal.

The setting of goals cannot be over emphasized. Without goals, your actions are directionless and haphazard. Even if you have a vague idea of what you want to get accomplished, you are more apt to run around in circles some before you actually start moving forward. A properly established goal gives you direction immediately. You can also use goals to measure progress. As we mentioned in the comparison of short-term and long-term goals, the completion of your goals should lead you to a better situation, which in itself is only part of an even *better* situation. You will accomplish various sub-goals in order to reach your larger goals, and these sub-goals tell you that you are making progress.

The word "business" is derived from the Old English word *bisig*, meaning "busy." The name implies movement and activity. When you set goals you create positive energy because you are creating *movement*. Everyone involved in reaching the goal realizes that they are moving to accomplish something. The goal is their destination.

What kinds of goals should a business or a partnership set? First, of course, the goals must adhere to the mission statement that was set earlier. Goals that are not in alignment with the mission statement go against the fundamental values that everyone agreed upon. In a case like that, support for the goal would be half-hearted, and there would be little chance of success. Besides that, the goals must be in alignment with the personal goals of the individuals involved. Partners may have varying personal goals, but the company's goals should be extensions of the individual goals that the partners themselves have set. Since the company is a part of their life, the company's goals should be a small part of their own personal goals.

If you try to get by without setting goals, you will soon find that the confusion and lack of direction take more energy to correct than does setting and fulfilling goals. Decision making is a challenge because every situation has to be evaluated on its own merits, without the benefit of guidance.

The process for setting goals can be broken down into simple steps. There are certain characteristics properly set goals have that make them more useful. We like to use the acronym SMART for our goal setting. SMART goals are those that are Specific, Measurable, Attainable, Risky, and Timely. By following these steps, you can make certain that you are creating goals that will benefit you and the company.

First, your goal should be **specific**. You want to focus your efforts for that one goal on a particular objective. For example, you wouldn't phrase your goal as "We want to build a new building and increase sales." The two points may both be valid and desirable, but they don't belong in the same goal. They are separate goals.

Specificity in your goal setting helps you conserve energy by cutting out extraneous activities that can distract you from your purpose. You also avoid confusion by having a single specific objective when you establish your goal. Our minds are not capable of effectively holding two thoughts at one time. By having the single thought of your goal, you create a clear vision of the accomplished objective in your mind, which makes you better able to achieve the goal.

The goals that you set must be **measurable**. The point of making them measurable is to answer this question: "*If you don't measure, how will you know when you're successful?*" There has to be a definite point at which you know that you have succeeded in reaching your goal. Once you reach that goal, you reevaluate and decide if you need to set another goal to take the place of the one you reached.

Another point of making your goal measurable is so you can celebrate when you reach it. You don't need a marching band and a parade, but when you reach a goal you should find a way to celebrate the occasion. If it's a small goal, a small celebration is in order. If you reached a more ambitious goal, then something a little larger might be called for. Celebrating your victories is a way to reinforce the pleasure of accomplishment. Just as you would reward someone else for doing a good job, you need to practice the same technique on yourself. While you may be a self-motivated individual, using positive reinforcement is a good way to keep your fires burning. Making your goals measurable helps remind you of when it's time to celebrate.

Your goals should also be things that are **attainable** through your own efforts. If you desire something to occur by chance or by luck, it's not a goal; it's a wish. For example, "winning the lottery" is not a goal. However, "saving money," properly phrased, would be a valid goal because it's something that is within your control. The reason you want your goal to be attainable is because reaching your goal will be something you accomplish. Reaching the goal is a process, and you have to be able to go through the process to make the goal a reality. Unless the goal is attainable, you really don't have a way to go through the process.

Your goals should also be **risky**. You do not want goals that are too easy to accomplish. Goals that are too easy to accomplish are not goals; they are tasks. Remember the saying "reach for the stars and you'll touch the moon." By definition, these goals are the ones for which you don't have hard data that guarantee success.

Based on your experience, intuition, and accurate assessment of your organization's potential, you should establish risky goals so that you can make the occasional leap over the competition and beyond what others believe is possible. History is full of visionaries who did the impossible. The Wright brothers had a goal of making a powered flying machine. Ray Kroc had a vision of creating a chain of affordable restaurants. John F. Kennedy had a vision of putting a man on the moon. Looking back, all of these accomplishments seemed inevitable, but at the time they were risky goals, attainable only through imagination and perseverance.

Every goal should also be ***timely***. Having a time limit on accomplishing your goal creates the sense of urgency that is sometimes required to get people moving. Without a time limit, no one would be in a rush to do anything, which in turn would likely mean that nothing would get done at all. The "sense of urgency" is what moves a goal to the top of the list of planned activities for the day. It doesn't mean that you should panic or that everything else must be set aside for that goal. It merely means that you have decided to assign importance to reaching the goal and to achieving it within the allotted time frame.

Finally, the goals that you set should reflect your priorities. Priorities are the items that will help your business reach the levels of success that you aspire to. Your actions reflect your priorities, making them a reality. *First things first.* So, as an example of a partnership goal, you might have, "Within the first three years of business, we will reach annual sales of five hundred thousand dollars." The goal is specific: annual sales. It is measurable: five hundred thousand dollars. It is achievable through your own efforts. It has a timeline: within three years. And, finally, it is a priority, if your values include sales as a priority. In the previous example, the goal would be risky if a comfortable annual sales goal was three hundred thousand dollars. Stretching it two hundred thousand dollars is risky but still achievable.

Goal-setting should be an ongoing process, as you achieve some goals and replace them with others. Always check and recheck your goals for conformity to your values and mission statement. When your goals, values, and actions are in agreement, you are on your way to a successful business partnership.

"Everybody is ignorant, only in different subjects."

~ Will Rogers

CHAPTER EIGHT

Whose Job Is It Anyway?: Divide and Conquer

One of the key benefits to a partnership is that the workload can be divided among the partners. Dividing responsibilities and holding each other accountable are keys to a healthy and successful partnership.

When deciding how responsibilities are to be divided, the partners must use proper communication techniques. Assigning areas of responsibility is one of the most important tasks that the partners can decide on together. It is vital that the concept of negotiation, thinking win-win, and working together to find acceptable roles are observed at all times. This is no time for one partner to bully another; one partner using such a technique can doom the partnership before it's even off the ground.

Within the business model, this is the time for the partners to honestly assess their individual strengths, weaknesses, styles, personalities, and preferences. Keeping this in mind, they can then work together to portion the areas of responsibility in the best manner possible. There may be areas that one or both partners find distasteful, objectionable, or unpleasant. If that's the case, some sort of compromise must be reached that is acceptable to both partners.

When assigning areas of responsibility, the partners should keep in mind the entrepreneurial and behavior styles discussed in chapter four. Based on those categories, some areas will be more acceptable and appropriate to a particular partner, while the other partner may be more easily assigned to other areas.

Deciding what all is involved in a business can stymie the entrepreneur. Especially when they're just starting out, there may be parts of the business that neither partner has taken into consideration. Not all companies will contain all the following areas of business, but each partner should be assigned control over the area that best fits their strengths. You never know when you might expand your business, and having the decision already made as to who will control something shows foresight and good planning.

Sales and marketing. The term *sales* refers to getting customers to buy your product or service. Marketing is an overall term that includes sales, but may also refer to advertising, promotions, or other activities to attract customers. Business guru Peter Drucker defines marketing as those activities that determine the target customer base and lead those customers to buy the company's product or service. All marketing activity, in other words, should be aimed at one result—a sale.

The type of activities necessary to engage in sales and marketing necessarily mean that the partner responsible for this area will come into contact with large numbers of people. Because of that, you would assign the partner who is a "people person" to this task—someone who is comfortable meeting new people and pleasantly engaging them.

Customer service. Every business needs a process in place to handle various situations with customers. It may be resolving customer complaints or answering questions for customers who are interested in the product or service the company offers. In either case, the situation needs to be resolved in a competent and professional manner.

This area requires someone who has detailed knowledge of the company's product or service. They would also need to have very good people skills so that they can de-escalate a situation in which a customer is unhappy. Often a customer whose complaint has been satisfactorily resolved can turn into one of the company's best customers.

Purchasing or buying. This area involves the purchase of products or supplies that the company needs in order to remain in business. It may involve buying raw materials which the business turns into the final product, items bought wholesale which the company then retails to customers, or supplies that the company needs to conduct business.

This area of responsibility is much, much more than simply spending money. In addition to knowing what the company needs to stay in business, the partner who handles purchasing must also forecast what the company's needs will be in the future. She must also know what the budget is and allocate funds appropriately so that there is enough product or supplies on hand for the business to function properly. Additionally, the purchaser must research and be aware of new products that can add to the efficiency and profitability of the business.

Operations. The term operations refers to the actual running of the business. In a restaurant, operations would involve the cooking and serving of food. In a dry cleaners business, it refers to cleaning of garments. In a garage, operations would mean working on vehicles. Operations is where the proverbial rubber meets the road; it's the reason the business, the company, and the partnership exist.

The partner in charge of operations must be the doer. She has to be the one who doesn't mind the day-to-day execution of the tasks around which the business is built. This can involve interacting extensively with employees and customers, so people skills are also required.

Personnel. Most businesses have employees. Those employees must be recruited, interviewed, hired, trained, and managed. It is also the responsibility of personnel to motivate, recognize, and reward outstanding performance. And, when performance is not acceptable, or company policy is violated, employees must be warned, reprimanded, or fired. These areas are the responsibility of the partner in charge of personnel. Obviously people skills are required for this job, but it also takes knowledge of the business (for training) and forecasting skills (to determine how many employees need to be hired), as well as interviewing and management skills.

The partner in charge of personnel must be in close contact with the partner in charge of operations, if they're not the same person. They must work together to ensure that the employees hired are capable of doing the job. Additionally, the partner in charge of personnel must be aware of laws surrounding employment discrimination, unions, or other requirements that may vary from state to state.

Accounting and clerical. Every business generates some sort of paperwork, if for no reason other than taxes must be paid. Obviously there are other requirements for which paperwork is necessary. While some chores such as accounting or bookkeeping are outsourced to third parties, the responsibility must ultimately lie with one of the partners.

This role requires some knowledge of general accounting principles, business law, and business reporting. One way or another, the partners need to know how their business is doing and whether they are making a profit or not. Clerical work, which some partners will find distasteful, must still be done.

Maintenance and repairs. The physical facilities of a business must be kept in working order for the business to operate. The equipment must also be in good shape. The responsibility for this must lie with the partner who has some knowledge of mechanics, carpentry, plumbing and other physical skills. The partner may not do the work himself, but he must be able to know when something is not functioning as it should.

Profits can be drained quickly if money is spent unnecessarily on preventable repairs. Maintaining a building or equipment can save money in the long run. Nothing is more disastrous to a new business trying to generate momentum than to be shut down because of equipment failure.

Warehousing and storage. Products and supplies that the company needs to stay in business must be stored somewhere, and they must be stored properly. This responsibility falls to the partner in charge of warehousing and storage. Knowledge of the products is imperative: Will they spoil? Will they rot? Do temperature extremes affect their quality? Are there hazardous chemicals involved?

General warehousing principles must also be part of the knowledge base. Such terms as "first in, first out" must be second nature to the partner in charge of this area. Knowledge of delivery schedules, holding times, and efficient use of space are all requirements for this responsibility.

Obviously, in a small company many of these duties will be handled by a single person. What is important, however, is that each partner minds her own area of control for which she is held accountable. Following such a principle leads to more efficiency and less conflict. Once a partner has accepted responsibility, the next step is to determine the amount of direct action the partner will take on the matter—in other words, how "hands on" the partner will become in ensuring that the task is accomplished. The task will either be done by the partner directly or *delegated* to someone else.

The art of delegation is a fundamental management skill that must be mastered by anyone who goes into business. Any kind of achievement will be much easier when a team is assigned to accomplishing it. Different parts of a task can be delegated to various team members, and the tasks can be executed concurrently, making it simpler to finish the task quickly.

Delegation also amplifies the power of the individual. By delegating lower priority tasks to other people, a partner can concentrate on accomplishing higher leverage goals. When high priority items are achieved, the business is successful. The partners are spending their time on consolidating or growing their business, perfecting procedures, or on other activities that increase cash flow and profits.

Literally, delegation is assigning responsibility to another person to get something done. When a partner is assigned a particular area of responsibility that has been delegated to them by the partnership, it does not necessarily mean that the partner is expected to achieve everything with their own hands. The actual tasks may be delegated to employees or outsourced.

One principle regarding delegation is that decisions and the carrying out of assignments should be done at the lowest level where the appropriate levels of knowledge, ability, and judgment are present. The subordinate (the person to whom a task is delegated) must have the information or knowledge required to carry out the task successfully. For example, if you ask your son to carry out the trash, he has to know where to take it. If he's five years old, he may not know, and thus delegating the task to him might be questionable. A teenager, on the other hand, can probably be counted on to go to the right place.

The individual also must have the ability to achieve the task. Our five-year-old from the example above may not be able to carry out a heavy metal trash can, but she may be able to handle a smaller, lighter plastic container. The same principle applies to asking an employee to do bookkeeping who has never had any training in accounting. The knowledge and ability are not there.

Most important is that the person to whom you delegate a task must have the judgment to achieve the task successfully. Sometimes the judgment is simply knowing when to ask for help. On more complex tasks, recognizing the appropriate decisions to make along the way are part of the responsibility. Someone who is more mature or experienced may be more qualified to accomplish the task rather than someone who is better educated.

So the first principle of delegation is to make sure that the person to whom you are delegating a task has the appropriate level of knowledge, ability, and judgment. Ignoring this principle can lead to disaster, especially on vital assignments. One caution: ability in one area does not necessarily translate to ability in another, unrelated area. Beware of the "halo effect"—assuming that a person is proficient in all things because of proficiency in one area—when delegating assignments.

Another principle of delegation is to be aware of what you are delegating. Depending on the level of delegation you are employing (we will say more on those in a moment) you must delegate *authority* (the right to make decisions necessary to accomplish a task) along with the *responsibility* (assuming the consequences for the completion of the task). Many times a poorly skilled manager will assign a high level of responsibility to a subordinate without assigning an appropriate level of authority. What you have then is an employee who lacks the decision-making power to complete the task but who will have to suffer if it is not done. The employee has been set up for failure.

Proper delegation involves making sure that the subordinate to whom the task has been delegated has the appropriate tools and support necessary to accomplish the task. This includes having the ability to make decisions that will affect the positive completion of the task. Giving someone the ability to make decisions in this manner is a great training ground to improve her judgment and confidence. A final principle is that items should not be unnecessarily delegated upward. In other words, tasks should be handled at the lowest level possible *when the knowledge, ability, and judgment are present.* Many times an employee will try to delegate something upward simply because she doesn't want to take the responsibility for making a decision. Lower-level routine decisions can be made by staff who are directly involved in the situation. The partner should not be making those types of decisions.

On the other hand, there may be times when it is important that the partner become involved in a task or decision that might otherwise be handled on a lower level. It may be important to make contact with a particular customer, for example. A partner may become a waiter for that particular customer so as to establish or reinforce a relationship. In other cases a lower level task may involve a delicate matter. For example, if a good customer has had bad service recently, the partner may take an active role in ensuring that the poor service is not repeated. Again, the personal attention shows that the matter is important not only to the employees but to the partners as well.

These examples illustrate that there are times when it is appropriate for a partner to handle lower-level chores directly. It may be simply to demonstrate to employees their willingness to "get their hands dirty." More often there are compelling reasons for the partner to do the chores. The danger is that the partner may become so busy doing lower level tasks and making low-priority decisions that higher-level priorities will be ignored.

As mentioned earlier, there are different levels of delegation. It pays for the partner to be aware of the different levels and to understand that each of the levels is appropriate in different circumstances. You have to use your own judgment to decide how much knowledge, ability, or judgment the subordinate has, so you can use the correct level of delegation.

Level One is "Don't do anything unless, and until, I say so." This level is hardly delegation at all. The partner spends almost as much time—maybe more time—working on the assignment as if he had done it himself. You have to investigate the situation yourself and determine what the conditions are so you can make the appropriate decision. This level shows a lack of trust in the subordinate's capacity to do the job.

Level Two is "Look into the matter, consult with me, and I'll tell you what to do." This saves a little time over Level One, but not much. The subordinate comes to you and tells you what the problem, decision, or task is, and you tell him what to do. This requires a lot of oversight from you, to make sure the employee does what you tell her to do.

Level Three is "Look into the matter, consult with me, and we will decide together what to do." This is a step up from the previous levels, and is the lowest level in which the subordinate has actual input. An employee can gain confidence from your having enough faith in her to respect her opinion.

Level Four is "Look into the matter, consult with me, and let me know what you're going to do." This level gives you veto power over a decision that might negatively affect the situation. At the same time, the subordinate is trusted to come to you with appropriate solutions.

Level Five is "Look into the matter, take care of it, and report back to me." At this level there is a high degree of trust in the judgment of the subordinate, as well as her ability to successfully accomplish the task. It may require verification on your part for legal or other reasons.

Level Six is the highest level of delegation. "Look into the matter, take care of it, no further contact necessary." When you can delegate an assignment in this matter, you maximize the time you can spend on higher-level priorities. Training employees to get them ready for this level of delegation should be one of your primary goals.

Delegation is not always to a subordinate. Businesspeople routinely hire professionals to do work for them: accountants to keep their books; lawyers to write up contracts; electricians, plumbers, and carpenters to maintain their buildings. The decision of whether to outsource a task to a third party may be part of the partner's responsibilities.

There are the normal questions of verifying the third party's expertise, proficiency, certification, etc. Some questions are peculiar to partnerships. For example, how much will using the third party cost? Is this within the budget of the partnership? Will the partners need to approve the expense beforehand?

When the partnership delegates responsibility to an individual partner, it may be a good idea to create certain limits on the responsibility. For example, expenses above a specified dollar amount require consulting with the other partner. Doing this can keep a budget from spiraling out of control. Especially when hiring an outside party to perform a particular function, limits must be set on the legal obligations a single partner is committing the business to.

All of the above situations are complicated when the partners are spouses. Trying to keep business and personal lives separate becomes a challenge in itself. However, thousands of couples work in their businesses together successfully, simply by following a few rules.

First, the couple must keep in mind each other's behavior style. One person may express himself dramatically, while the other is quieter. One person may be "bookish", while the other is more outgoing and people-oriented. Neither partner should try to force the other into an unnatural style simply because the business needs it. Spouses should be allowed to conduct themselves in their own way.

It's also important to clarify and define job roles at home and at work. While every partnership requires job definition regarding the business, it is even more important that roles be spelled out clearly when spouses are involved. There is often bleed-over from home to business and vice versa. This can be detrimental to both.

At work, first resolve that any personal issues will be handled privately, as separate from the business as possible. Next, there needs to be some sort of understanding about how business is conducted. Is one spouse the working partner, and the other the "owner's spouse?" Or are both partners heavily involved in operations at the jobsite?

There must also be agreement as to how instructions to employees are carried out. When the partners send different messages to employees, the resulting confusion can hurt the business. There must be some understanding beforehand as to how employees are to be treated and how information is distributed to them.

Ultimately, the decision about who's the "boss" at work needs to be made. Single reporting relationships are a fundamental management principle. If employees have something to discuss with "the boss," they need to have a single person in mind. The decision as to who that person will be must be negotiated by the spouses beforehand. Such preparation can make the business run smoother.

Just as important is answering the question "Who's the boss at home?" While most households and marriages are cooperative, the time commitment necessary to run a successful business may keep one spouse out of the house more than is normal. In that case, the other spouse must take on responsibility to ensure the smooth running of the household. If he is not willing to do that, then there can only be trouble at home.

One main point to keep in mind: family is always first. While imbalances are normal and necessary when starting a new business, there should never be a case where the family suffers because of the business. Keeping family first helps every businessperson maintain their equilibrium. When stress at work becomes unbearable, they should be able to replenish their energies by engaging with their family.

Time away from work is when you refresh yourself. If you find that you can't concentrate on having fun with your family because of business concerns, or you no longer take pleasure from being around them, then your priorities have become distorted. It's time to reorganize your life so that your family is a source of inspiration and energy for you.

This means that you must dedicate time to your children. One of your motivations should be to provide a better life for them. "Better life" does not mean giving them money. It means being there when they need you and participating in their lives. If you have to leave work to attend a ball game, then do it. The return on your investment will be larger than anything your business can provide.

The End of a Partnership (Dan)

In 1999 we expanded our retail holdings by opening a magic and joke shop in a local shopping mall. The plan was to expand the concept into other shopping malls throughout the country.

We had the business experience and the capital but did not have the time to operate this business solo. We selected a husband-and-wife team to be our partners because they had previous experience in operating magic shops in shopping malls. They did not have money, but they did have the time to devote to the day-to-day operations of the business. In addition to being friends, they also shared our vision and desire to build a retail magic empire.

We did not have a written partnership agreement or charter. However, we did verbally agree on each of our roles and responsibilities. I was the financial investor and the owner of the business, so my income was the profit. They had the title of manager and ran the day-to-day operations. They worked for a pay check.

Unfortunately, the time came where we were not meeting our sales expectations. In fact, we were losing quite a bit of money. Out of frustration, I stormed into the shop one day and demanded that we make some major operational changes. I reprimanded my managers for doing things that were not helping the business get out of its financial slump. How could such knowledgeable people become so incompetent? The business was losing money and they were doing nothing to fix the issues.

They did comply with my requests to make the changes. However, the next day they both quit. This project was their dream too, and over night they lost interest. I did not want to continue this project without a suitable partner, so I eventually shut it down.

What went wrong with this partnership? The error was communication or, more specifically, lack of communication. Looking back, I have to admit that I did not communicate effectively with my managers. I simply let them operate the business and I expected a profit. They had many ideas that they wanted to implement. However, I was not accessible, so many of their ideas were never considered or implemented. I did not share the seriousness of the income losses to my managers, so they had no clue that I was losing money. Because they were not aware of the financial situation of the business, they assumed everything was fine. All of us failed to communicate effectively.

Without a proper game plan and good communication, when a business takes a financial downturn it can destroy both the partnership and the relationship.

"Promises and pie crusts are made to be broken."

~ Jonathan Swift

CHAPTER NINE

Read All About It: Creating Partnership Charters and Agreements

Although partnerships are based on relationships, and relationships are between people, there are times when paperwork can actually benefit relationships, and so partnerships. If you are a person who dislikes paperwork, you may be pleasantly surprised by how helpful some documents can be.

A partnership is a matter of understanding. Two people come together for a particular purpose and propose to join their resources and energy to create a business that will benefit both of them. Their understanding is that they have the same goals for the business and that they both want it to be successful.

If running a business stopped there, then there would never be any need for documentation. Every transaction could be handled with a handshake. Alas, this perfect world does not exist. Pressures mount, other people offer opinions, and life in general rocks the lives of the partners. The possibility for conflict and disagreement escalates. Soon the partners forget all the noble dreams with which they created the partnership, and they can focus only on the problem that is bothering them.

When this happens, it helps to have documentation to help remind the partners of what they had in common at the beginning and what they understood their situation to be. This documentation can take two forms: a partnership agreement or a partnership charter. Both can serve as reminders of what the partners agreed to, but each in very different ways.

A *partnership agreement* is a legal document that commits the partners to particular obligations. It gives a legal definition of the partnership; the partners; and the type of business they are entering into, including every minute detail of the business side of the partnership. The partnership agreement is a legally binding contract that the partners enter into.

If the partnership begins to fail for some reason—one partner fails to fulfill his obligations, for example—the agreement is presented as evidence in a court proceeding, and judgment is made as to whether one or both of the partners violated the contract. In other words, the agreement is punitive.

Rather, it *can* be punitive. As with any legal move, a partnership agreement only serves as a reminder—a rather strict reminder—of what obligations each partner is required to fulfill. When the partners do as they have agreed, the agreement is an idle, inert object that has no bearing on the business. It may be used to nudge a recalcitrant partner into line, but behind the "nudge" is the threat of legal action.

What the partnership agreement does is simplify the course of action when various circumstances arise. The other partner or partners can take appropriate legal action and the matter is decided in the most expeditious manner possible. The agreement has spelled it all out for the courts.

The *partnership charter*, on the other hand, is a living document that provides for the well-being of the partnership from the outset. Whereas the partnership agreement provides legal recourse if a partner *fails* to fulfill his responsibility, the partnership charter can *help* the partners fulfill their duties.

A partnership charter is a written document in which the roles, responsibilities, values, and various other elements of the partnership are spelled out. They are a working guide to help the partners get along with one another, to facilitate communication, and to provide guidance for the partners.

One point is important to note here. The document itself is not as important as the conversations that precede the partnership charter. The process of creating the charter can result in some of the warmest, most enlightening conversations businesspeople ever have with one another.

For example, when discussing the business values, the partners may have to engage in soul searching and introspection to discover what their own values are. They exchange this information with their other partner, and in doing so they learn more about each other, more than many people share with close friends. This introspection and self-examination can lead to a greater insight as to what type of person they are and what type of person they want to be.

Many people are not trained to be partners. The partnership charter is designed to provide a blueprint for them to follow. The development of the charter provides a chance for them to learn about the business as well as about their partner and themselves. They may find that there is much more to owning and running a business than they thought. For this reason, a partnership charter is good for entrepreneurs who are starting their first business.

There are some cases, however, when a partnership agreement, with all its legalities, is the best course. Experienced businesspeople who have been partners in other businesses already know what's expected of them. Especially if they have partnered with the same people previously, a partnership charter would be redundant for them and would serve no useful purpose. A simple legal document is all they need to get started.

The advantage of the partnership charter is that it provides a structure to address issues that can make or break a partnership. A good partnership charter will cover three key areas: business issues, relationship issues, and future issues. Business issues are those topics that pertain specifically to the company itself. Encompassing several areas, the charter should specify exactly what situations might arise and how they should be handled. Following are some areas that the charter should cover.

Roles and responsibilities. As we have discussed earlier, each partner has particular strengths and weaknesses. The partnership charter is where the assignments should be spelled out. The partner for each area of the business should be assigned, as well as exactly what they are responsible for. Whenever there is a conflict about whose job a given task is, the charter can be referred to as the ultimate resource.

It often helps to spell out *limitations* in the charter. Approval of purchases over a certain dollar amount, for instance, may be necessary to keep the budget in line. If the limits established at first prove to be unrealistic, the partners can always change the amounts by agreeing to amend the charter. If a partner does not understand, or forgets a particular responsibility, the partners can refer to the charter for clarification.

Obligations. Besides the legal obligations, this is where the informal obligations are to be found. It may turn out that each partner must contribute a certain dollar amount regularly to the business. The partners may agree to forego taking any profit until the business has a substantial emergency fund established. There may be other more individual obligations that would be spelled out in the charter.

Values. The charter is where the underlying beliefs and attitudes of the partners would be expressed in the business. As a partner you want your business to express a certain point of view toward life and toward people. These company values may be as basic as committing to provide top-notch customer service. They may be more specific—working to improve the environment, for example. In any case, the charter can be the place where you explicitly state the values that the partners use as a guide in making business decisions.

Goals and mission statement. Goals are the ultimate objectives of the business and how the partners measure their success. The mission statement goes beyond goals and expresses the attitude and values the company and the partners will adhere to as they strive to reach their goals. Whenever a decision needs to be made, the partners should be able to look to their mission statement and determine what course to follow.

Goals can be monetary in nature, of course, but they can also express much more. A goal may be any milestone when, upon reaching it, the partners can celebrate the success. It might be something as simple as earning an award for being a great corporate citizen. The main thing to keep in mind is that a goal should be something that the partners can celebrate after they reach it.

Relationship issues are those items which determine how the partners interact with one another. There are almost an infinite number of circumstances that could be addressed here. The following are just a few of the possible issues.

Interactions. Interactions are any time the partners have any sort of dealing with one another at all. It may be face-to-face conversation, talking over the phone, or even just being together in the same space. A charter can specify concerns that the partners have about communication styles or how they address one another when in front of employees.

This is an area where forethought can avoid problems. Discussing the subject in detail when there is no stress leads to better, more creative solutions. A partner may be sensitive about being treated respectfully and not care for horseplay or playful nicknames. Such topics as these can be addressed over a series of conversations, with the reasons behind the suggestions explained. The conversations often lead to understanding, and understanding leads to better partnerships.

Personal conduct. The conduct of the partners, whether during business hours or not, can affect the partnership. If a partner engages in activities that reflect poorly on the business, the entire enterprise suffers. The charter can take this into consideration and spell out what is acceptable behavior and what is not.

Adults have the freedom to live their lives as they wish, but they also have to take the consequences for their actions. If a partner feels that a charter restricts his life too much, then he must consider if he should enter into the partnership at all. In many ways, the partnership takes priority over other parts of the partners' life. A compromise may be necessary for partners to be satisfied with charter requirements regarding personal conduct.

Handling conflict. Since we have determined that some conflict is inevitable in a partnership, it makes sense if the partners prepare for it beforehand so that they can limit the damage it does. The charter is the perfect place to spell out the process for resolving conflicts. The partners should understand that they will be held to a mature standard and that by doing so they will be helping the partnership.

If facilitation, mediation, or counseling is part of the process, then the partners can use the charter to determine who will be the ones that they turn to for help. They can also reinforce their commitment to putting the partnership first and agree to abide by the process that they put in place. By simply agreeing to the process, they are avoiding potential conflicts.

Future issues. It's impossible to know in advance every potential event that might happen. What the partnership charter can do, however, is establish guidelines that the partners can follow in the event of certain conditions in the future. One future situation that the partnership charter can prepare for is when, for one reason or another, there is a change in ownership of the business. Although the partners go into the business with the intention of staying partners, it's a good idea to address certain issues if something happens that makes a change inevitable. The prior planning of the charter can make transitions in the ownership dynamic smoother and less intrusive to the business.

The first possibility is that there may be a major shift in the roles and responsibilities of the partners. Such a shift may be the result of several different conditions. One of the partners may be attending college and becomes certified in a profession during the partnership. The agreement may be made in advance that upon the graduation, that partner takes over a more prominent role.

Another, more dramatic possibility is that one of the partners has proven to be incompetent or unable to fulfill the responsibilities called for by the partnership. The process for determining this must be set up in advance if there is not to be damage to the business. When the shift in responsibilities occurs, it needs to be done with a minimum amount of fuss. Reorganization can be hard on employees as well as the partners, so it must be done quickly, efficiently, and professionally.

When the partners are spouses, the death of one of them, or a divorce, can tear apart a business. Besides the personal stress the remaining partner goes through when a spouse dies, the business can fall apart if there is no contingency plan for operation. When multiple partners are involved, the burden is eased slightly but must still be addressed. Whether it is separation, divorce, or a death, provisions must be expressed in the charter as to what actions will be taken to resolve the situation. If spouses separate or divorce and choose to continue being business partners, there will have to be guidelines outlining acceptable behavior and defining the legal ramifications that their divorce will have on the business.

Sometimes a partner will want to cut back on his involvement with the business. This may be for a variety of reasons—the partner may have health problems that limit his abilities; he may be involved with another venture that requires more of his attention, and will thus seek to lessen his involvement with this one; a partner may wish to semi-retire and pursue personal goals.

In all of these cases, one thing remains: there will have to be a reorganization of the duties, roles, and responsibilities of the remaining partners. The charter can delineate the process that the one partner needs to follow to make the transition smooth, as well as how the remaining duties, etc., will be assigned.

The partners will also need to determine if a partner who wishes to cut back on his involvement is entitled to the same amount of proceeds from the business or if he will be allowed to remain a partner at all. Some businesses require a heavier commitment of time and energy from every partner, and when one reduces his involvement, the load can be excessive for the remaining partners. It may be better in some instances for the partner to leave the business completely so that the others can find a replacement. This is the type of decision that the partners can make in advance and enter into the partnership charter.

The same principle applies when a partner chooses to retire. Depending on the level of involvement in the business, the duties that the partner was responsible for, and similar questions, a solution for the situation must be determined. If this is done in advance using the charter, the damage to the business is minimized.

The charter is also the place that the partners can express their respect and affection for one another. One way is to award a percentage of the partnership to the retiring partner as a pension or added source of income, even though the partner will not be active in the partnership. This is a very personal decision for each of the partners and can be a way for the partnership to reward its members for a lifetime of work. Whether this type of plan is followed or not, it's evident that such situations must be addressed.

A seemingly similar, but fundamentally different, situation occurs when one of the partners wants to quit or simply quits. This could be as dramatic as walking off the job or as quiet as the partner expressing his wishes in a memo. A partner wanting to quit can be a result of many different situations. However, it is usually an indication that he is unhappy with something that has transpired in the business.

Obviously, if the partner is involved in operations and simply walks out, damage is done to the business and to the partnership. If the relationship and communication between the partners has deteriorated to this point, then it is time to completely reassess the dealings between the partners. Although not common among professional people, quitting without notice still happens.

More common is that the partner will express his desire to no longer be associated with the business. Depending on the company's financial situation, the compensation—if any—to be paid to the partner should be determined in advance, in the charter. This amount may be determined by the method the partner chooses when quitting: walking out in the middle of operations may leave the departing partner with nothing, whereas advance notice may lead to a healthy sum.

In any of the cases, the charter can be used to make the transition as smooth as possible as well as to maintain the relationship between the partners. There may be stress involved in this type of transition, when decision making and communication may not be at their highest levels. Better to do it in advance by including the process in the charter.

One aspect to keep in mind is when the quitting partner wants to sell their share of the business. The charter is the place where that process can be explicitly stated. For example, the remaining partners may have the right of first refusal—in other words, they get the first chance to buy the quitting partner's interest in the business. The charter may also determine the compensation that the quitting partner is entitled to, depending on the situation.

The remaining partners may also reserve the right to approve the sale of ownership of the business. For whatever reason, there may be instances when the partners do not want the quitting partner's sale to go to a particular party or individual. If the remaining partners will have this right, the charter is the place where that right, as well as its limits and boundaries, is expressed.

Even more problematic is when a partner engages in unethical or illegal behavior. As mentioned earlier, such behavior not only affects the partner who engages in it, it also reflects on the business and the other partners. To protect the business and the reputations of the other partners, the charter should address what happens when illegal or unethical behavior occurs.

First, though, there needs to be a definition of exactly what constitutes "illegal" or "unethical" behavior. The mere accusation of poor behavior should not necessarily disqualify the partner from ownership and control of their share of the business. There have been numerous occasions when someone has been accused of a particular act, only to later be found innocent of any wrongdoing.

So the definition of the behavior should be defined. When a partner is accused of a crime, for instance, is action taken when he is arrested? When he is indicted by a grand jury? When he is convicted? Depending on the severity of the alleged crime and its impact on the partners' ability to conduct business, any of these levels may be appropriate.

When the crime has been committed against the business—embezzling, for example—the procedure may need to be different. The consequences may need to be swifter and more severe so as to minimize the damage to the business. There may need to be a probationary period where the partner is removed from all operations until an investigation has been conducted.

If it appears that the accused partner will go to jail, or will be otherwise removed from active participation in the partnership, it may be necessary for his share of the business to go to someone else. Again, the charter can determine if his share reverts to the remaining partners and, if so, how compensation is determined.

While perhaps not as severe as violations of the law, unethical behavior can cause a company's reputation to become tarnished, thus damaging the business. Again, definitions of unethical behavior—perhaps based on the values and mission statement included in the charter—can be spelled out, as well as the consequences. A variety of reactions is possible. It may be as simple as a series of increasingly severe reprimands (oral, written, official, for example) to requiring the offender to get counseling or attend classes on business ethics.

Additionally, the reaction to the behavior must be based on the level of certainty and verification that the alleged behavior actually occurred. It is imprudent and unproductive to punish someone for behavior that it turns out they were not guilty of. The process that determines the level of verification needed before an official reaction by the partners must be clearly spelled out.

Finally, the charter should list in detail the process to follow upon the death of one of the partners. Besides defining the legal aspect (reassignment of the partner's shares, accommodating the will, etc.) it may be desirable to devote some time and space in the charter to expressing the feelings of the partnership toward the deceased. For example, it may be put in the charter that upon the death of a partner, the partnership will send flowers or, on the other end of the scale, pay for the full cost of the funeral. That kind of decision should be preplanned, so that if and when it occurs the emotion of the moment does not overwhelm judgment.

A Partnership That Went Bad (Dan)

As a real estate investor and landlord, I have owned dozens of residential rental properties throughout the United States. In the 1980s I was actively buying residential and commercial real estate in Colorado.

I created what I thought was the perfect partnership with a real estate broker. I had the operational skills but no money. He had the ability to find great investments and he had money.

Our partnership agreement was simple. He would find a real estate investment, and I would buy it. Since he was a real estate broker, he would receive a nice commission check each time he sold property to me. He carried his commission as a second or third position loan on the property, and on many occasions he would lend me an additional 5 to 10 percent toward the down payment on the property.

In every situation, I was the sole owner of the real estate, and I was responsible for all operations, operating costs, and future capital investments. I was the landlord working toward long-term capital gains. He was merely an investor holding notes on dozens of properties; receiving nice residual income. This was a win-win situation for both partners.

In addition to this exciting business partnership, we were great friends. We thought we were invincible. I was sitting on a real estate goldmine. Even though my properties were highly leveraged, I was experiencing a 0 percent vacancy rate. I was receiving plenty of rental income—enough to cover my mortgages and enough to pay my partner his interest.

Everything was great until the economy deteriorated and the real estate market crashed in Colorado in 1988. Almost overnight I was facing a 40 percent vacancy rate. Tenants moved out. Many tenants could not pay their rent. New tenants were few and far between. Within a year I was financially sinking. I was unable to pay all of my debts, and I couldn't pay my partner.

I lost all of the properties through foreclosure and eventual bankruptcy. My partner lost thousands of dollars in commissions and cash investments. The partnership was over. This is how two friends become enemies. I blamed him for selling me properties just before the market turned, and he blamed me for letting the properties go into foreclosure.

A business partnership is a business venture and does involve an element of risk, including loss of finances, personal credibility, friendships, and relationships. Those not willing to put these on the line should be very careful who they partner with or they should consider going solo.

"I always wondered why somebody doesn't do something about that. Then I realized I was somebody."

~ Lily Tomlin

CHAPTER TEN

What Goes Around, Comes Around: Giving Back

Motivational speaker Zig Ziglar has said, "You can get everything you want in life, if you help enough other people get what they want." Winston Churchill said, "You make a living by what you get. You make a life by what you give."

Throughout this book we have emphasized the importance of articulating your values in your business. We have illustrated how conducting your business according to your values can lead to a better business, along with more sales and profit. This chapter, however, is about giving back—giving back to your customers, to your community, and to society.

For many years, small businesses have been confronted with the challenge of getting their message out among the huge volume of information and advertising. Customers have been so inundated with messages in every conceivable medium that they have become used to a constant barrage of advertising "noise."

In this environment, a small business has to do something extraordinary to get customers' attention. A method that many have found to be extremely successful is the practice of being a good corporate citizen, of volunteering and giving back. A business derives a multitude of benefits from participating in the community.

One result many entrepreneurs don't expect is that they improve the balance in their personal life. How does giving back add balance to your life? First of all, it breaks the cycle of work that many ambitious business owners fall into. They find reasons to keep working, and they slowly become buried in their work, unaware that they are sacrificing their personal lives in their pursuit of success.

Volunteering and helping others gets entrepreneurs away from the business. It provides a new outlook, one in which they fill a different role. When they assume a new role, they often take the opportunity to reassess how they fill other roles such as mother, father, husband, wife, family member.

When you help others, you also provide a valuable lesson to your children. They understand that if we are to be good members of society we each have an obligation to help others in whatever way we can. This is not a lesson that they can learn from you in your workplace. The classroom for teaching your children about giving is away from your workplace.

Giving back also teaches you another type of lesson: the pleasure of helping others. When you are working long days and nights to make your business more profitable and to attract new business, you can get into a very me-oriented state of mind. Helping others is the exact opposite of that mindset and can be the activity that keeps you from becoming too absorbed in your own personal interests all the time.

It's important that each of us contribute to society in whatever way we can. American culture has become used to accusations of selfishness because so many of our activities and interests are self-centered. However, a defining characteristic of Americans since the country began more than two hundred years ago is the willingness to serve and to help the community.

According to the U.S. Department of Labor, about 61 million people volunteered with an organization at least once during a recent year. That translates to about 26.2 percent of the American population who served as volunteers. These volunteers spent a median of 52 hours a year working with their organizations to help others. Clearly Americans understand the concept of helping others, a direct refutation of the "selfish" label. Individuals, however, can still be selfish. It is this trap that you want to escape—a trap you may have fallen into in your quest to make your business successful.

How do you decide in what way to give back? Look around. Is there something that's important to you? Is there a problem that's been bothering you? Maybe there's a section of street in your town that is full of potholes; find a way to get them repaired. Maybe there is a shortage of crossing guards at your children's school; volunteer to help out in the afternoons. The personal implications of your service may be more important to you than anything else. You may have a child who suffers from a particular disease or condition. You can find an organization that addresses this very personal part of your life and volunteer to help them. If there's not someone already doing it, you may start your own campaign.

Another way to decide how to give back is to see what's needed. Does a local telethon need phone volunteers every year? Do they have enough volunteers but need food and refreshments? You can only find the answer to these questions by looking around and talking to people.

Another consideration is what you are in a position to do. Your business provides a valuable service; see how you can use that advantage to help out. It might be as simple as providing coupons for your services for an organization to raffle or give away. You may be able to get your employees to volunteer for activities where more people are needed.

There are of course economic benefits to your business for volunteering. You become more visible, in a way that leaves a positive impression on your customers. Some companies pay thousands of dollars trying to create an image of their business that you could get for free simply by volunteering.

The next question that needs to be answered is, naturally, *How do I get started?* The easiest answer to that is, join! Depending on your personality, this may be easy or hard for you. Your partner may be a people person who is already a member of a large number of groups. You, on the other hand, may be the quiet type who prefers being alone or with a small number of friends.

If you feel challenged to join a group, try to understand that your help will be appreciated by whichever organization you choose to join. There is always more need than there is help, so your additional support will certainly be of great benefit, wherever you go. You can help in whatever way you feel most comfortable, but you won't get that chance until you actually join. It's not enough simply to join, however. Anyone can become a member on paper. You must volunteer to help. An active volunteer is always put to good use. Your attitude toward volunteering will favorably impress people, and that image will help your business.

If your organization does not have anything going on for which you can volunteer, express a willingness to start something or to help someone else get a project started. Many times leaders in an organization are simply waiting for someone to step up and say they are willing to help. Your openness may be the catalyst that gets a project started.

Next, you will need to answer the question "*Who do I partner with?*" There are any number of groups and organizations where you can get started. The first choice for many people is through their religious affiliation. According to the Department of Labor report mentioned earlier, more than a third of all volunteers perform their duties through a religious organization. These organizations generally have a large number of volunteer opportunities—everything from teaching Sunday school to babysitting for working mothers to working at car washes. Most religious organizations have a built-in system that supports its members helping. They make it as easy as possible for volunteers to put their energy to good use. Another common volunteer need is in schools and other educational entities. Schools are always looking for volunteers and private monetary donations.

There are service groups in most cities or towns. You can often go to the yellow pages of your phone book and look under the listing for "Civic Organizations" and find multiple listings. Service groups exist for the express purpose of helping the community and helping society. They are constantly seeking new members to help with their projects.

Some of the civic groups you may have heard of are Lions Clubs International (www.lionsclubs.org), Rotary International (www.rotary.org), or the League of Women Voters (www.lwv.org). These are just a few examples; there are of course hundreds more. Find a volunteer organization that has the spirit of giving and helping others that you are looking for. We provide information for some examples of civic groups and charities at the end of the chapter.

You may be more interested in helping with youth groups such as the Girl Scouts or Boy Scouts. There may be a Boys' or Girls' Club nearby where you can volunteer. If you are an active person who likes to have fun, this may be your best route. Your activities will be geared toward children and teenagers, so you know it won't be boring! Your own children may benefit from your joining such a group. If they have not joined before, this may be the opportunity they need to approach a group and become a member. They will reap the benefits of being part of an organization and will start learning what it's like to be a volunteer who helps other people.

There may be community projects that need help. The potholes mentioned earlier are a good example. Other projects are more oriented toward development and progress rather than repair, and that may appeal to you more. Read the newspaper to see when a committee or group is being formed to address a particular issue. See if that group can use your help.

One acquaintance of ours saw the large number of skateboarders on the sidewalks and in parking lots and decided to do something for them. He approached the city to see about building a skateboard park for the kids. The city told him they would pay for half the cost of building the park if he could come up with the rest. He began his own campaign to raise funds, even arranging for a circus to visit. The skateboard park was built, and the skateboarders could do their tricks without endangering pedestrians.

Another possibility is to look for political affiliations to partner with. You may have a pet cause—environmentalism, for example—that you feel needs promoting. You can volunteer to help organizations and political figures who promote your cause. You likely would meet a lot of people, and often do a lot of walking, as you go door-to-door seeking support for your position.

The true magic of partnering with an organization is that it provides the avenue for you to make a HUGE difference in the world around you. Working with like-minded people who have similar goals multiplies the results of your efforts exponentially. A team of organized, committed individuals who work toward a common goal is powerful. Organizations that are formed for a particular purpose provide a means for caring individuals to work together to multiply their results in ways that none of them could do alone. The whole truly is greater than the sum of its parts.

Regardless of the cause that you care to join and support, remember that being a true partner involves more than simply "doing your time." You are developing relationships that can be meaningful to other people as well as to yourself. Those relationships should be precious to you, and you should care for them accordingly.

Giving back to society is a concept that has been wrapped in philosophy and moral teachings for a long time. Only in recent years has it become a standardized part of how business should be done. Volunteering and giving don't lend themselves to a formula that you learn in business school, but they can become a part of your business education if you let them.

The new rule for businesses is not earning gold, it's conducting your business by following the Golden Rule: *Do unto others as you would have others do unto you.*

Civic Organizations and Charities

American Cancer Society (www.cancer.org) 250 Williams Street, Ste. 600, Atlanta, GA, 30303

The American Cancer Society is a nationwide, community-based voluntary health organization. Headquartered in Atlanta, Georgia, the ACS has state divisions and more than thirty-four hundred local offices. With chartered divisions throughout the country, the ACS is committed to fighting cancer through balanced programs of research, education, patient service, advocacy, and rehabilitation. The Relay For Life is a major fundraising program of the ACS. There are thousands of Relay For Life events held each year throughout North America and around the world. Where ever you live, there is probably a Relay event held nearby. For more information visit www.relayforlife.org.

The American Red Cross (www.american.redcross.org) P.O. Box 37243, Washington DC, 20013

This humanitarian organization, led by volunteers and guided by its *Congressional Charter* and the Fundamental Principles of the International Red Cross Movement, provides relief to victims of disaster and helps people prevent, prepare for, and respond to emergencies.

The Association of Junior Leagues International, Inc. (www.ajli.org) 80 Maiden Lane, Suite 305, New York, NY, 10038

This is an organization of women committed to promoting voluntarism, developing the potential of women and improving communities through the effective action and leadership of trained volunteers. Its purpose is exclusively educational and charitable.

Civitan International (www.civitan.com) P.O. Box 130744, Birmingham, AL, 35213

The mission of Civitan worldwide is to build good citizenship by providing a volunteer organization of clubs dedicated to serving individual and community needs with an emphasis on helping people with developmental disabilities.

Kiwanis International (www.kiwanis.org) 3636 Woodview Trace, Indianapolis, IN, 46268

The name "Kiwanis" means "we trade" or "we share our talents." It was coined from an American Indian expression, Nunc Kee-wanis. Kiwanians are volunteers changing the world through service to children and communities. Kiwanis members help shelter the homeless, feed the hungry, mentor the disadvantaged, and care for the sick. They develop youth as leaders, build playgrounds, raise funds for pediatric research, and much more.

League of Women Voters (www.lwv.org) 1730 M Street NW, Suite 1000, Washington, DC, 20036

Despite its name, the LWV is not limited to women. The League of Women Voters, a nonpartisan political organization, has fought since 1920 to improve our systems of government and impact public policies through citizen education and advocacy. The League is a grassroots organization, working at the national, state, and local levels. There are Leagues in all fifty states, the District of Columbia, Puerto Rico, the Virgin Islands, and Hong Kong, in addition to the hundreds of local Leagues nationwide.

Lions Clubs International (www.lionsclubs.org) 300 West 22nd Street, Oak Brook, IL, 60523

Formed in 1917, the association of Lions has provided millions of people with the opportunity to give back to their communities. Lions is an international network of more than a million men and women in over two hundred countries who work together to answer the needs and challenges of communities around the world. Known for working to end preventable blindness, Lions participates in a wide variety of projects important to its communities. These projects range from cleaning up local parks to providing supplies to victims of natural disasters.

Optimist International (www.optimist.org) 4494 Lindell Boulevard, St. Louis, MO, 63108

This organization is serious about "Bringing Out the Best in Kids" and doing their part through community service programs. Since each Club is autonomous and run by members in their communities, Optimists have the unique flexibility to serve the youth of their community in any way they see fit. Optimist Clubs see a need in their community and react to it.

Rotary International (www.rotary.org) One Rotary Center, 1560 Sherman Avenue, Evanston, IL, 60201

Rotary is a worldwide organization of more than 1.2 million business, professional, and community leaders. Members of Rotary clubs, known as Rotarians, provide humanitarian service, encourage high ethical standards in all vocations, and help build peace and goodwill in the world. There are thirty-three thousand Rotary clubs throughout the world in more than two hundred countries and geographical areas. Clubs are nonpolitical, nonreligious, and open to all cultures, races, and creeds. As signified by the motto *Service Above Self*, Rotaries main objective is service—in the workplace, in the community, and throughout the world.

Soroptimist International (www.soroptimistinternational.org) 1709 Spruce Street, Philadelphia, PA, 19103

This is a worldwide organization for women in management and professions working through service projects to advance human rights and the status of women. The website includes the World Span newsletter and extracts from The International Soroptimist magazine.

United Way (www.liveunited.org)

This is a national network of nearly thirteen hundred local organizations that work to advance the common good by focusing on education, income, and health. United Way declared these to be the building blocks for a good life: a quality education that leads to a stable job, enough income to support a family through retirement, and good health.

VolunteerMatch (www.volunteermatch.org)

This organization is a leader in the nonprofit world dedicated to helping everyone find a great place to volunteer. VolunteerMatch offers a variety of online services to support a community of nonprofit, volunteer, and business leaders committed to civic engagement. Its popular service welcomes millions of visitors a year and has become the preferred internet recruiting tool for more than 61,000 nonprofit organizations.

The International Volunteer Programs Association (IVPA) (www.volunteerinternational.org)

This is an alliance of nongovernmental organizations involved in international volunteer work and internship exchanges. IVPA can serve as a guide to anyone considering volunteering abroad or developing international service opportunities. This includes but is not limited to prospective volunteers, newly created volunteer sending organizations, corporations, and colleges and universities.

"You cannot have everything. I mean, where would you put it?"

~ Steven Wright

CHAPTER ELEVEN

Know When to Say When: Partnership Nirvana

After owning, operating, failing, and succeeding in many business and partnership experiences, we believe one of the simplest partnership concepts to succeed in is not the traditional "brick-and-mortar" business. The simplest partnership concept is to operate a home-based business. With a home-based business, your operating costs are minimal, compared to a traditional brick-and-mortar business. It is also convenient to partner with a spouse, family member, or friend. Depending on the business concept, you may also partner with customers, clients, or other home-based business owners. And, of course, you will partner with the company that provides you with your products and services.

There are hundreds of reputable home-based business concepts that are partnerships you can operate, including internet marketing companies such as eBay or Amazon. Other home-based concepts include network marketing, multi-level marketing (MLM), direct marketing, and referral marketing companies. These concepts are business partnerships in the truest sense of the word. Most network marketing companies are designed so that you share revenue with one or more people in the organizations network when you purchase, sell, or refer others to purchase the products or services. The people that make money from your efforts (often referred to as up-line, trainers, or leaders) support you and help you succeed, because they succeed if you succeed. They are your partners.

The marketing concepts described above are a partnership nirvana. Each person is eager to help everyone else in the business network because they all have a vested interest in each other's financial success. This type of partnership business model is simple to implement with minimal start-up costs. Like any business start-up, it is highly recommended that you research any company you are considering partnering with. Most home-based business companies are legitimate. However, do your due diligence and get referrals from their current partners and clients. Also, scrutinize the product or services the company offers. Are the products of high quality, competitively priced, and unique? How does the company stand, financially? How long has the company been in business? Do they have debt? Are they profitable? Are sales growing or declining?

If you currently own or manage a business, you can create a similar partnership nirvana. Develop a profit or revenue sharing plan with your employees and managers. When one employee succeeds in a sale, receives a bonus, or gets a promotion, extend the revenue sharing with everyone in the department. If implemented properly, and consistently, employees will support and help each other because there is something in it for each of them. You will create a work culture of teamwork and partnership.

"We didn't lose the game; we just ran out of time!"
~ Vince Lombardi

CHAPTER TWELVE

All Things Great and Small: Putting the Tools Together

In this chapter we'll review what's been presented in the previous chapters and put all the tools together into a cohesive package that works for you. In chapter one, "The Business Partnership Dilemma," we discussed the pros and cons of going into business and whether or not you should have a partner. Also, we redefine what a "partner" is, or can be.

Getting into business can be relatively easy. The government tries to create conditions so that small businesses can start up, helping fulfill the American dream. If you have a hobby that you enjoy, you could turn it into a business. You may have a skill or knowledge that you picked up on your job or in the course of your life. They can be turned into a service business that you do either part-time or full-time.

Owning a business is a tremendous responsibility. The lives of many people, many *families* are in your hands. If your business fails, you are not the only one who suffers. An entire support structure made of people will suffer along with you. By starting your business, you take on the responsibility of providing for each of them in some way. Just as you depend on each of them for their individual contribution, they each depend on you and have an investment in your success. They have restructured their lives and their obligations for your benefit.

Getting out of business may not be easy. There are legal, financial, and personal concerns to consider when trying to liquidate a business. When you enter into a partnership, the complications are multiplied. It is wise to ask some questions of yourself before you take on a partner:

- Why do you want to own a business?
- Why do you want to have a partner?
- Are there alternatives to taking on a partner?
- Is the person you are choosing the best partner for you?
- After you choose partners, are all partners in agreement on how to get out of business?

In chapter two, "Partnering with Family," we learned that taking on family members as partners has tremendous benefits, but we must also watch out for potential pitfalls.

One question to ask may surprise you: exactly who is "family?" The relationship you have with various members, especially in this day of blended families, single parents, and extended relationships, will vary.

Problems arise from trying to maintain a relationship, run a household *and* run a business all at the same time. Meticulous planning and preparation combined with maturity and understanding are key.

Luckily, there are tools, techniques, and strategies available for working with your family as partners. Regarding tools, remember to *put it in writing*. Legal documents and signed paperwork are not absolute safeguards, but they beat having nothing at all. The purpose of having documentation of all agreements, assignments, and responsibilities is not necessarily to produce them in a court of law. If a dispute has gotten that far, the damage to the relationship is already done. Rather, documentation is designed to remind partners—even family members—of what they agreed to beforehand.

Useful strategies include exercising open communication and being aware of stress levels. With open communication, resentment and other negative emotions are dealt with quickly, before they have a chance to take root. Personal slights, often a result of a misunderstanding, are one of the most common causes of difficulties in a partnership. Talking openly about emotional matters often heads off trouble before it starts.

Stress can kill a partnership, just as it can kill a person. With family members, you can often see the signs of stress before they are aware of it themselves. This is one of the times where your familiarity with your partner really pays off. When you see the signs of stress, communicate with them and find out if there is a problem.

Useful strategies for successful family partnerships include:

- Keep personal and business matters as separate as possible
- Structure and plan your activities to purposely prevent bleed-over between personal life and business life
- Involve extended family members in your business to prevent resentment and jealousy

There are three main types of entrepreneurial couples: the solo entrepreneur with a supportive spouse, the copreneurial couple, and the "dual entrepreneurial" couple. All of them have various advantages, but you have to decide which arrangement works best for you and your partner.

In chapter three, "Partnering with Business and Industry," we learned a new definition of a partner as a *stakeholder,* or someone who has an interest in the success of your business. You discovered various ways to turn others into stakeholders in your company. You can turn someone into a stakeholder by:

- Sharing profits
- Sharing business
- Sharing credit
- Sharing customers

One type of partnering relationship is the franchisor–franchisee relationship. Many of the most successful entrepreneurial businesses have been franchises. There are various benefits and drawbacks to the franchise system. You get name recognition, established procedures, marketing support, and more. On the downside, you have to share your profits with the company and lose some of your independence and autonomy. There are organizations that can help you run your franchise or help you decide if you want to franchise at all.

Other partnership possibilities are with vendors, customers, service and trade organizations, and even other businesses. There are also the benefits of co-branding, finding affiliate partners, or working with advertising co-ops. The important thing regarding business relationships is to consider all areas of your life and look to establish partnerships rather than to just "do business" or "have a relationship." By working toward making each interaction win-win, you develop partners who will help you and your business become successful.

Are there business models out there that are already doing what you want to do? Find out what it takes to partner with them. The franchisor–franchisee relationship is a perfect example of such a partnership. Partnerships are the key to successful business interactions.

In chapter four, "Defining Entrepreneurial and Behavioral Styles," we found ways to discover our tendencies in different key roles in the partnership. Almost any personality type can start and run a successful business, as long as the entrepreneur understands his personality—his strengths and weaknesses—and incorporates techniques and tools that play to his strengths while minimizing weaknesses.

The four basic behavior styles are Controller, Promoter, Supporter, and Analyst. The Controller tends to be competitive, the go-getter, the one who works to get things done. Controllers can also be abrasive, task-oriented, and short on people skills.

The Promoter has the natural ability to motivate and inspire--both themselves and others. The Promoter tends to be imaginative and creative in getting desired results. Unfortunately, because of their quick decision making, Promoters are guilty of poor planning and lack of follow-through.

The Supporter is the ultimate team player. The Supporter can be counted on to do what's necessary to help everyone win. They are more likely to listen to what others are saying rather than crave the spotlight. A possible downside is that the Supporter may avoid confrontation and resist change.

The Analyst is detail oriented. Every organization and company needs an Analyst. They have the patience to examine the details of a plan and point out any weaknesses. Unfortunately, he may also have perfectionist tendencies and suffer from "paralysis by analysis."

This synopsis is a simple way to remember the characteristics of each behavior style. The Controller makes sure the goal is achieved; the Promoter plans the party so everyone can celebrate; the Supporter makes sure everyone gets recognized at the party; and the Analyst figures out how to pay for the party.

Entrepreneurial style is important also. Partners can work together and maximize their effectiveness if they are aware of each other's dominant entrepreneurial style. There are four basic types of entrepreneurial styles: the All-Rounder, the Organizer, the Routiner, and the Pioneer.

The All-Rounder is the universally responsible entrepreneur, the dynamo who has her fingers in every part of the business. The All-Rounder seems to know something about everything. Unfortunately, this may lead to an inability to delegate effectively.

The Organizer is the one who will create a business plan and apply for all the licenses, certifications, etc., that the business needs to run. The Organizer makes sure that resources are put to their best use. Rational, logical, and able to think things through, the Organizer figures out which direction the business needs to go.

When you have an entrepreneur who has small business goals and takes every step carefully, you have the Routiner. The Routiner is likely to operate businesses that have a proven track record or which have very low startup costs. Caution directs all of the Routiner's decisions because she knows that a misstep can be expensive.

The Pioneer is the visionary, the one who usually comes up with the initial idea for a business. The Pioneer may be drawn to entrepreneurship because she wants to have the satisfaction of having her vision realized. The Pioneer is an innovator—a dynamic, creative entrepreneur.

In chapter five, "Effective Communication Strategies," we learned about the importance of good communication and discovered strategies that can add to our effectiveness and to the success of the partnership.

Communication is *when the meaning of what you want to convey to another person is completely and accurately transmitted and received.* Although it sounds simple, the definition hides a multitude of possible obstacles to communication.

Communication is more than simply talking and listening. Although effectively using those two skills will improve your communication drastically, they are just a small part of the arsenal you can bring to good communications. Unfortunately, most people have not even mastered those two skills.

We use communication to transmit ideas. However, even two people who are extremely close, who have a great affinity for one another, can have communication breakdown sometimes, when they simply can't understand one another. The idea—the meaning, the entire package of emotions, images, consequences, and causes—simply isn't coming through clearly.

At its most fundamental level, most communication is a face-to-face conversation between two people. In that one simple conversation, there are a number of methods of communication being used. First you have the words being spoken. Each word has a particular dictionary definition or *denotation*. But words also have *connotation*, the second meaning or subtext that accompanies the denotation. The connotation of language refers to the emotional impact that the word causes in the listener.

Body language such as gestures and facial expressions are also important in communication in person. With written communications, although body language is not applicable, there are still subtexts that can be determined based on the language and word choices.

In business communication, it's a good idea to keep all conversations on a professional level that pertains to business matters. With a spouse or relative, this may be difficult, but it's important to make the attempt. One similarity in both personal and business communication, however, is that when there is a strain, communication is the first thing to suffer. In both instances keep an eye on the level of communication, and that can tell you if there are other problems that need to be addressed. Of course, the only way to discover what those problems are is by *communicating*.

When problems arise, open and effective communication can solve them before they get out of hand. Some ground rules to keep in mind when communicating:

- **Stay on the subject**. No good comes of bringing up grudges from the past while trying to resolve the current issue.
- **Listen for understanding**. To be sure that you are staying on the subject, you have to actually listen to what the other person is saying.
- **Adapt your behavior**. Be flexible by adapting your behavior to ensure that you're both staying on the subject.

Listening well is one of the keys to effective communication. As Stephen Covey says, "Seek first to understand, then to be understood." Listen for the emotion underlying what's being said, as well as to the words.

Talking for understanding is when you take into consideration the other person's behavior style, her interests, and the effect your words have on her.

There are four primary learning styles: Auditory, Visual, Kinesthetic, and Auditory-Digital. Understand what style your listener's primary learning style is and try to communicate with her in a fashion that complements her style.

In chapter six, "Confrontation and Conflict Resolution," we learned techniques that successful entrepreneurs use to resolve conflicts with their partners. Although there are many ways to get *into* conflicts with partners, there are only a few ways to get *out* of conflicts.

There is a spectrum of conflict resolution possibilities. Find and use the one that is acceptable to both parties and which involves the least amount of disturbance to the partnership:

- **Negotiation**. The preferred method of conflict resolution
- **Facilitation**. Negotiation with the help of a third party
- **Mediation**. Both partners present their cases to a third party who makes a recommendation
- **Counseling**. The partners seek the help of a professional counselor for advice

- **Expert advice**. The partners seek the advice of an expert
- **Arbitration**. Mediation by a third party that is legally binding
- **Litigation**. The last resort. Involves the legal system, courts, and lawyers

In most cases, negotiation is all that's needed to resolve a conflict between partners. Regardless of what method the partners use to resolve the conflict, there are some guidelines that need to be observed.

1. Agree on and clarify all the issues in dispute.
2. Emphasize that each person has ample opportunity to share his opinions.
3. Collect facts and data.
4. List the pros and cons of each person's position.
5. Identify alternatives.
6. Come to an agreement or consensus on what represents the best solution.

The foundation for effective conflict resolution is the willingness to compromise. It's not a mature, or realistic, expectation to get your way 100 percent of the time. It's not even realistic to expect to get 100 percent of your way *most* of the time.

Persuading your partner into submission is not an effective method in resolving conflict. The partner who has been "persuaded" may simply be eager to escape the argument. The persuaded partner merely feels bullied. Although the confrontation itself has been resolved short-term, the spirit of partnership has been damaged.

A successful partnership thrives when the partners:

- Are willing to compromise and consider other points of view
- Demonstrate flexibility and are open to change
- Share common goals
- Respect and support each others decisions

When it comes to actually handling a conflict, language is the most important —and potentially devastating—tool that you have at your disposal. Especially when you are passionate about a subject, it's vital that you choose your words wisely to avoid unintentionally hurting your partner. Remember that it's the situation you want to attack, not the other person.

Negativity will destroy a partnership. It brings shame to the partner who introduces it and can shame a partner who retaliates with it.

An effective partnership is a three-legged stool, supported by open communication, honesty, and trust.

The way we view conflict illustrates how we view life in general. If you view conflict as a win-or-lose competition between partners, then someone will inevitably suffer because of it. If you think of conflict as a way for you to grow, for you to temper the steel of your character, then conflict resolution can benefit your personal life tremendously.

Chapter seven, "Values, Missions, and Goals," is where we learned the fundamentals of establishing a value statement, a mission statement, and how to set goals for your partnership and company.

Every company has values, whether they are explicitly stated or not. Values are the standards of behavior that the business—employees, partners, and representatives—follows when it conducts business. Values are the standards you want to adhere to in all of your actions. They are like instructions for behavior when you don't have precise instructions. They are the moral laws that everyone in the business should follow when they start to do something.

A *value statement* is a written expression of corporate morality, the values that the company holds most dear. The value statement is the foundation upon which all decisions and actions of the business are based.

Once a value statement has been created, the next step is to create a *mission statement*. A mission statement is the expression of those values in action. The mission statement is an unchangeable belief system that the members of the organization can count on and refer to when they have a question about a course of action. The mission statement is a reference guide, a place everyone can look to for direction and instruction. It serves as a guide to acting on values. It answers the question of "how will we embrace our values in the business?"

After the establishment of your mission statement, it's time to work on your goals. Just as your mission statement was based on your values, your goals need to be based on your values *and* your mission statement. By establishing your goals from the bottom up like this, you can proceed confidently, knowing that you won't run into an ethical conflict anywhere along the way. Remember that *goals are the execution of the expression of your mission statement and your values.* Goals are values in action.

One way to classify goals is by their timeframe. Long-term goals are strategic and may range over months or even years. Short-term goals may be measured in days, weeks, or months.

The process for setting goals can be broken down into simple steps. By following the steps, you can make certain that you are creating goals that will benefit you and the company. Well-constructed goals will have the following characteristics:

Specific. Specificity in your goal setting helps you conserve energy by cutting out extraneous activities that can distract you from your purpose.

Measurable. "*If you don't measure, how will you know when you're successful?*" Making your goals measurable helps remind you of when it's time to celebrate.

Achievable. The reason you want your goal to be achievable is because reaching your goal will be something you accomplish. Reaching the goal is a process, and you have to be able to go through the process to make the goal a reality.

Risky. You do not want goals that are too easy to accomplish. Goals that are too easy to accomplish are not goals; they are tasks. Remember the saying "reach for the stars and you'll touch the moon." By definition, these goals are the ones for which you don't have hard data that guarantee success.

Timely. Having a time limit on accomplishing your goal creates the sense of urgency that moves a goal to the top of the list of planned activities for the day. And don't forget to prioritize. Priorities are the items that will help your business reach the levels of success that you aspire to. Your actions reflect your priorities, making them a reality. Put first things first.

Goal-setting should be an ongoing process as you achieve some goals and replace them with others. Always check and recheck your goals for conformity to your values and mission statement. When your goals, values, and actions are in agreement, you are on your way to a successful business partnership.

Chapter eight, "Divide and Conquer," dealt with how to assign various roles and responsibilities to the partners. Dividing responsibilities and holding each other accountable are keys to a healthy and successful partnership.

Assigning areas of responsibility is one of the most important tasks that the partners can decide on together. It is vital that the ideas of negotiation, thinking win-win, and working together to find acceptable roles are observed at all times. When assigning areas of responsibility, the partners should keep in mind their respective entrepreneurial and behavior styles. Some areas will be more acceptable and appropriate to a particular partner, while the other partner may be more easily assigned to other areas.

Some of the areas that are part of a working business include:

Sales and marketing. The term *sales* refers to getting customers to buy your product or service. Marketing is an overall term that includes sales, but may also refer to advertising, promotions, or other activities to attract customers.

Customer service. Every business needs a process in place to handle various situations with customers. It may be resolving customer complaints or answering questions for customers interested in the product or service the company offers. In either case, the situation needs to be resolved in a competent and professional manner.

Purchasing or buying. This area involves the purchase of products or supplies that the company needs in order to remain in business.

Operations. The term operations refers to the actual running of the business. It is the operations where the proverbial rubber meets the road. It's the reason the business, the company, and the partnership exist.

Personnel. Employees must be recruited, interviewed, hired, trained, managed, and recognized. In some cases, employees must also be fired. These areas are the responsibility of the partner in charge of personnel.

Accounting and clerical. Every business generates some sort of paperwork. While some chores such as accounting or bookkeeping can be outsourced to third parties, the responsibility must ultimately lie with one of the partners.

Maintenance and repairs. The physical facilities and equipment of a business must be kept in working order for the business to operate. This responsibility falls under the domain of the partner in charge of maintenance and repairs.

Warehousing and storage. Products and supplies that the company needs to stay in business must be stored somewhere, and they must be stored properly. This responsibility falls to the partner in charge of warehousing and storage.

It is vital that once a partner has accepted responsibility for a particular area they be held accountable for that area.

Delegation is a key concept in management. It refers to getting work done through other people. Effective delegation can multiply a partner's effectiveness. Poor delegation will only add to the burden. It is important that if you delegate responsibility for a task, that you also delegate the authority necessary to accomplish the task.

There are various levels of delegation possible.

- Level One - "Don't do anything unless, and until, I say so."
- Level Two - "Look into the matter, consult with me, and I'll tell you what to do."
- Level Three - "Look into the matter, consult with me, and we will decide together what to do."
- Level Four - "Look into the matter, consult with me, and let me know what you're going to do."
- Level Five - "Look into the matter, take care of it, and report back to me."
- Level Six - "Look into the matter, take care of it, no further contact necessary."

Job assignment is more complex when the partners are spouses. They must juggle home and business without adversely affecting either of them. The key rule to remember is that family is always first. You must dedicate time to your children. You work to improve their lives, and very often you do that by spending time with them.

Chapter nine, "Creating Partnership Charters and Agreements," provided details on why it's important to create a written record of expectations *before* you dive into a partnership. It also gives tips on how to create your own partnership charter.

A partnership agreement is a legal document that commits the partners to particular obligations. A partnership charter helps the partners fulfill their duties. In this document, the roles, responsibilities, values, and various other elements of the partnership are spelled out. They are a working guide to help the partners get along with one another, to facilitate communication, and to provide guidance for the partners.

Many people are not trained to be partners. The partnership charter is designed to provide a blueprint for them to follow. A good partnership charter will cover three key areas: business issues, relationship issues, and future issues.

Under the heading business issues, you found the following items:

Roles and responsibilities. The partnership charter is where the assignments for the various partners should be spelled out. The partner for each area of the business should be assigned, as well as exactly what he is responsible for.

Obligations. Besides the legal obligations, this is where informal obligations are to be found.

Values. The charter is where the underlying beliefs and attitudes of the partners would be expressed.

Goals and mission statement. Goals contain the ultimate objectives of the business and are a guide by which the partners measure their success. The mission statement goes beyond goals and expresses the attitude and values the company and the partners will adhere to as they strive to reach their goals.

Under relationship issues you might find the following:

Interactions. Interactions occur any time the partners have any sort of dealing with one another.

Personal conduct. The conduct of the partners, whether during business hours or not, can affect the partnership. The charter spells out what is acceptable behavior and what is not.

Handling conflict. The charter spells out the process for resolving conflicts.
The charter establishes guidelines the partners can follow in the event of certain situations in the future. One potential future situation that the partnership

charter can prepare for is when, for one reason or another, there is a change in ownership of the business. If this happens, the charter can guide the partners and help them make appropriate decisions.

In chapter ten we discussed "giving back." This chapter suggests the importance of giving back to your customers, to your community, and to society.

As an entrepreneur, finding balance in life is a daily struggle. Giving back through financial contribution and volunteerism is an effective way of improving the balance in your life. When you help others, you also provide a valuable lesson to your children, and you receive the pleasure of helping others. There are also economic benefits to your business for giving and volunteering. You become more visible in a way that leaves a positive impression on your customers.

When your company is ready to start giving one question to ask is "*Who do I partner with?*" There are any number of groups and organizations where you can get started. The first choice for many people is through a religious organization. Another choice is through schools and service groups. There are service groups in most cities or towns. You can often go to the Yellow Pages and look under the listing for "Civic Organizations" and find multiple listings. Service groups exist for the express purpose of helping the community and helping society. They are constantly seeking new members to help with their projects.

The true magic of partnering with an organization is that it provides the avenue for you to make a *huge* difference in the world around you. Working with like-minded people who have similar goals multiplies the results of your efforts exponentially.

The new rule for businesses is not earning gold, it's conducting your business by following the Golden Rule: *Do unto others as you would have others do unto you.* The last chapter suggests partnership nirvana with home-based businesses. The simplest partnership concept is to operate a home-based business. With a home-based business, your operating costs are minimal compared to a traditional brick-and-mortar business. It is also convenient to partner with a spouse, family member, or friend.

Chapter eleven talked about partnership nirvana. There are hundreds of reputable home-based business concepts that involve partnerships you can operate, including internet marketing companies such as eBay or Amazon. Other home-based concepts include network marketing, multi-level marketing (MLM), direct marketing, and referral marketing companies.

Putting all of these activities, guidelines, and processes together is not for the faint of heart. Those who decide to pursue their entrepreneurial dreams and take on partners are hearty souls. What these suggestions will do, though, is help make the establishment and running of a business easier, more profitable, and more pleasant. By following the guidelines we've discussed, a partnership can last indefinitely, with all partners prospering.

About the Authors

Dan and Manon Rodriguez—with their passion for creating and building business ventures—have a unique approach to harnessing relationships and partnerships in the business world. Over the past twenty-plus years, they have owned and operated McDonald's Restaurants, multiple rental property investments, a Martinizing Dry Cleaning franchise, and a host of other retail and service businesses.

Despite their varied business background, these busy entrepreneurs thrive on their ability to work together, both as spouses and as business partners. Their approach to developing successful relationships and strategic partnership alliances has earned them respect in the communities in which they do business.

Dan Rodriguez is the author of several business-related books and is a small business expert specializing in business partnerships. He is a successful real estate investor, entrepreneur, public speaker, and lecturer. Since 1980, he has presented over five thousand lectures, workshops, and keynote speeches throughout the United States. As a veteran of the stage, Dan is also a professional magician and, in 1993, served as national president of the Society of American Magicians, the oldest and most prestigious magic organization in the world. Neither television nor radio are foreign to Dan; he has been interviewed on over one hundred radio and television stations, and has hosted a daily television talk show.

Manon Rodriguez is a sought-after expert in the employee development and human relationship field. She has earned numerous recognitions as an entrepreneur and business leader in the restaurant industry. During her tenure as a McDonald's franchisee, she was a founding member and division chair of McDonald's People First Initiative—the program McDonald's currently uses to train and recognize outstanding employee performance. In addition to her success as a business owner, public speaker, lecturer, and consultant, Manon is a strong supporter of giving back to the communities in which she does business. She has held volunteer leadership positions with many nonprofit organizations, including Rotary International and the American Cancer Society.

The authors continue to work tirelessly in the business world—always creating new ventures and business partnerships. However, their focus has shifted to motivating, teaching, and consulting with others who want to grow and prosper in the business world. This book is one step in that shift.

Dan and Manon Rodriguez have been married together for more than 20 years. Their children are Tara (and son-in-law Steve), Colin, Stephen, and Miranda, and are proud grandparents of Jackson Daniel.

The authors feature an informative and entertaining presentation that is available for your organization. For more information, visit: www.anythingwithtwoheads.com

Notes